NELSON ESSENTIAL HISTORY SKILLS

RUTH **NAUMANN**
MARYELLEN **DAVIDSON**

SECOND EDITION

Nelson Essential History Skills
2nd Edition
Ruth Naumann
Maryellen Davidson

Publisher: Tanya Wasylewski
Project editor: Aynslie Harper
Editor: Sylvia Marson
Text designer: Astred Hicks
Cover designer: Ruth O'Connor
Permissions researcher: Wendy Duncan
Production controller: Julie McArthur
Typeset by: Q2A Media

Any URLs contained in this publication were checked for currency during the production process. Note, however, that the publisher cannot vouch for the ongoing currency of URLs.

For product information and technology assistance,
in Australia call **1300 790 853**;
in New Zealand call **0800 449 725**

For permission to use material from this text or product, please email **aust.permissions@cengage.com**

ISBN 978 0 17 036714 1

Cengage Learning Australia
Level 7, 80 Dorcas Street
South Melbourne, Victoria Australia 3205

Cengage Learning New Zealand
Unit 4B Rosedale Office Park
331 Rosedale Road, Albany, North Shore 0632, NZ

For learning solutions, visit **cengage.com.au**

Printed in Malaysia by Papercraft.
6 7 24

CONTENTS

HISTORICAL INVESTIGATION

ISBN 9780170367141

UNIT 1
WHAT IS HISTORY?

History = the study of the past; for example, the story of your life until now is *your history*

History comes from *historia*, a Greek word meaning 'knowledge obtained by enquiry'.

The 'Father of history' is Herodotus. He lived in ancient Greece and died about 425 BCE (**B**efore the **C**ommon **E**ra). He wanted to find out what caused a war between the Greeks and Persians (Persia is the old name for the country of Iran). So he travelled around the area and asked questions. Then he wrote down the events and tried to explain why they happened. That is the first history we know about.

Sometimes students groan when they hear the word 'history'. They think history is a collection of dates they have to learn off by heart. But dates can be important. For example, you will use the date on which you were born many times throughout your life. History is many things. Even historians argue about its meaning, just as fiercely as they argue about historical events and people. One thing history is about is 'finding things out'. For example, your history class might go to a local museum, dress up in period costume and do historical activities, such as churning butter to make scones, then eating them. History is also about examining what has changed over time.

1 Write down four differences between you and Herodotus.

a ______________________________

b ______________________________

c ______________________________

d ______________________________

2 Write down four activities that you do today that your grandparents did not do or did differently.

a ______________________________

b ______________________________

c ______________________________

d ______________________________

3 In the box, write or draw what *history* is.

ISBN 9780170367141

UNIT 2

WHAT HISTORICAL INFORMATION MEANS

Historical information is about historical facts (something that can be proved; see also Units 25 and 46).

information = knowledge gained through experience or study

Example: One of Kip's ancestors was 13 years old when she was transported from England to the convict settlement in Australia for trying to steal bread to feed her family. Kip knows this because the event was recorded in official documents, in the front page of the family bible that has been handed down the generations, and on a family tree made by a professional genealogist.

Historical information is also about historical ideas (something you realise or understand after you have checked out all the facts).

Example: Demetre had Greek ancestors on one side of his family. He had heard them talk of the dark days of the Second World War. In his History class, Demetre learnt that Italy and Germany invaded Greece. Because they were part of the Allies, Australians were fighting against Italy and Germany. The 6th Australian Division went to Greece and helped the Greeks defend their country. The Greeks welcomed them as heroes. In his History class, Demetre also learnt about Crete and that it is a Greek island. Germany sent in parachutists and planes in a huge air attack. Waiting to fight them in Crete was an Allied force. It had Australians in it. The people of Crete were grateful. Demetre now had a good understanding of an historical idea – that the historical relationship between Australians and Greeks was good. The Greeks today still remember that soldiers from Australia came to help them in those difficult days.

1 Name two things that historical information is about.

a ______________________ b ______________________

2 Finish the following to give two pieces of historical information about yourself.

a When I was young, I watched ______________________

b Earlier this year, I went to ______________________

3 Give four historical facts you have learnt in this unit.

____

____

4 In the box, write or draw what *historical information* is.

UNIT 3
WHERE HISTORY HAPPENS

All around the world, right now, history is being made.

History happens everywhere. This is why historians need to know where places and countries are.

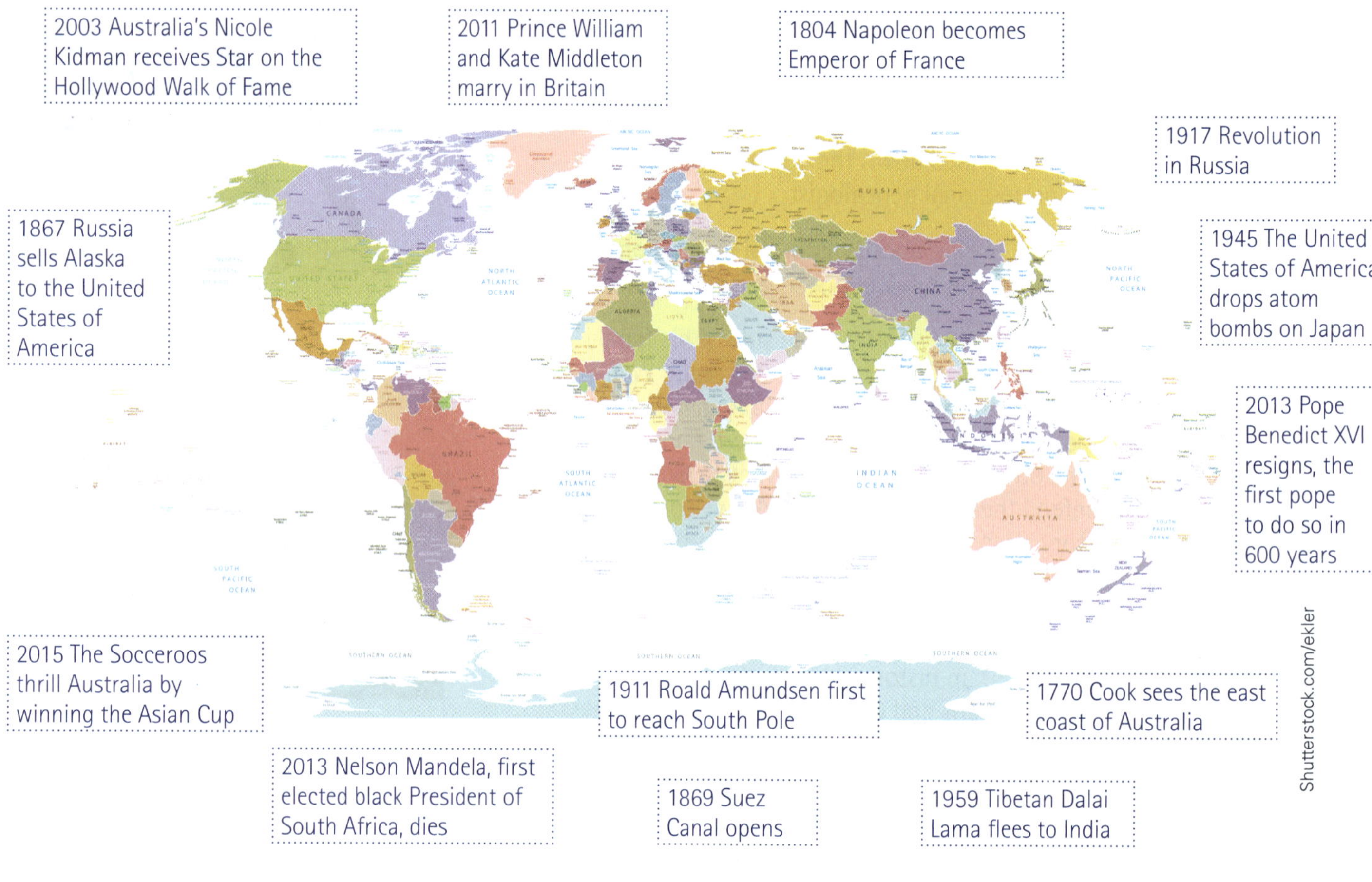

Shutterstock.com/ekler

1 Give the date, time, place and country in which you are sitting at this moment. Add a comment about why that time is now history.

____

____

2 Draw arrows from the boxes to the places on the map where the events happened.

3 In the box below, write or draw why it is important to know *where history happens.*

ISBN 9780170367141

UNIT 4
MAPS CHANGE OVER TIME

Maps change as a result of natural activity and human activity. Geological or climate change results in changes in sea levels, continental drift and the advance and retreat of ice sheets. For example, at one time, Japan was attached to the eastern coast of the Eurasian continent. It is now separate and made up of a number of islands. Borders can change through human political actions, such as when one country defeats another in war. Borders can also change when countries have been absorbed into empires, or new countries have been formed with new names in the aftermath of a war. The latter happened in Europe after the First World War.

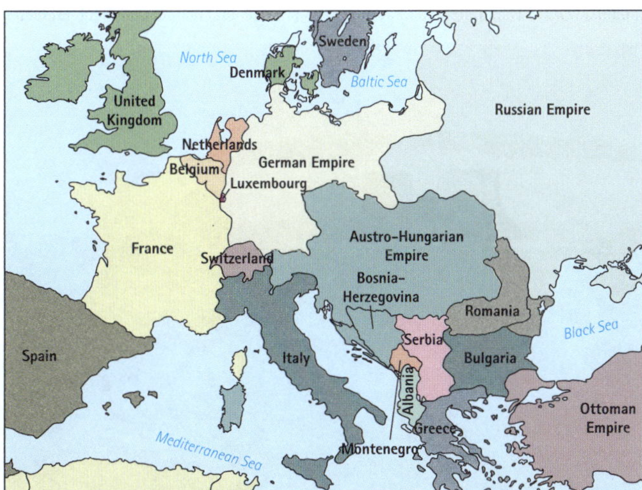

Map A: Map of Europe in 1914 before the First World War

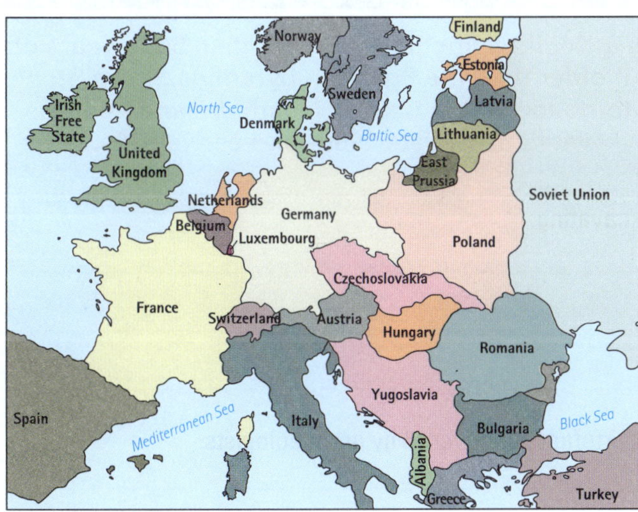

Map B: Map of Europe in 1925 after the First World War

1 Describe the changes in the maps from 1914 to 1925. Your answer should name the countries and empires that have disappeared and the new countries that have appeared.

______

______

2 Write why it is important to know the changes to maps.

______

______

3 Can you name two countries in Europe that started fighting over territory in 2013? ______

UNIT 5
WHAT IS ARCHAEOLOGY?

archaeology archaeo = ancient + ology = the study of

Archaeology is the scientific study of humans who lived in the ancient (prehistoric) and recent past through an examination of the material remains left behind. These artefacts or remains are the sources for the archaeologists and can date from any period.

Archaeologists record and interpret remains that include buildings, burial mounds, bodies, clothes, weapons, pottery, jewellery, fossils and shipwrecks. These are often discovered by excavating (digging) sites where people are thought to have lived.

From these sources, archaeologists select historical information that they use as evidence for their ideas about the past. When interpreting evidence, archaeologists use knowledge from other subject areas such as art, science, forensics and medicine.

Archaeologists focus on an examination of objects that can come from societies and cultures that have no written language, while historians examine written records and documents.

Knowledge about the ancient past increases with new methods such as carbon dating and dendrochronology (the term used for tree-ring dating). Changes in climate can also increase our knowledge of the past. In 1991, Otzi, the 5000-year-old 'Iceman', was discovered after the ice thawed on a mountain between Austria and Italy.

author photo

Newgrange is a Neolithic monument more than 5000 years old, which makes it older than the Egyptian pyramids. It is a Stone Age passage-tomb located in County Meath, Ireland and was extensively excavated in the late 1960s and early 1970s.

1 Write down three sources that archaeologists find by excavating.

a ____________________

b ____________________

c ____________________

2 Name two new methods of dating monuments and other artefacts uncovered by archaeologists.

____

____

3 Name two other subject areas from which archaeologists can draw knowledge to help them investigate new discoveries.

____

____

4 What is the difference between historians and archaeologists?

____

____

____

ISBN 9780170367141

UNIT 6
THE 5Ws AND H OF HISTORY

History answers, or tries to answer questions about:

WHO e.g. Who did the Australian Socceroos beat to win the Asian Cup in 2015? *(Republic of Korea)*
WHAT e.g. What word was used for the prisoners transported from Britain to Australia? *(convicts)*
WHERE e.g. Where was rapper Eminem born? *(Kansas City, USA)*
WHEN e.g. When did the Great Depression begin? *(1929 Wall Street Crash in the USA)*
WHY e.g. Why is Australia Day celebrated on 26 January? *(26 January 1788 is when Captain Arthur Phillip landed and claimed New South Wales as a colony of Britain)*
HOW e.g. How did your family come to be living in this country and not somewhere else?

HOW is the extra one to the 5Ws; it adds information such as:

'in what manner', e.g. How did Elvis die?

'in what condition', e.g. How was Elizabeth I's state of mood after she had Mary, Queen of Scots executed?

'to what extent', e.g. How many wives did Henry VIII have?

'at what price', e.g. How much did the 2000 Sydney Olympics cost Australia?

'for what reason', e.g. How did the Nazis come to power in Germany?

iStockphoto/HultonArchive

Mary, Queen of Scots

WHY   WHAT

WHO   WHEN

One of the first places that the Boxing Day tsunami of 2004 hit was an island near Sumatra. It swept away thousands of people, including 13-year-old Meghna. She survived in the ocean for two days by clinging to a door. She knew in which direction the land lay, so she floated towards the shore. Helicopters failed to spot her. Finally, the waves washed Meghna ashore. She was badly bruised and dazed. Locals found her and took her to hospital where she recovered.

WHERE   HOW

1 Fill in the missing answer to HOW to show how your family came to be living here.

2 Draw arrows from the 5Ws and H in the tsunami story to show to which bits of the story they refer.

3 The rhyming verse below, about the 5Ws and H, is from a famous story writer named Rudyard Kipling (1865–1936). Work out what the three missing words are most likely to be and write them in.

> I keep six honest serving men
> They taught me all I knew
> Their names are What and Why and ______________
> And How and ______________ and ______________

4 In the box, write or draw what *historical information* is.

UNIT 7
SOCIAL HISTORY

iStockphoto/Robert Churchill

Some people think history means just studying governments. Or wars. Or famous leaders. But history is also about ordinary people and ordinary society at different moments in the past.

Social historians look at all the different types of people you may meet, such as any of the following.

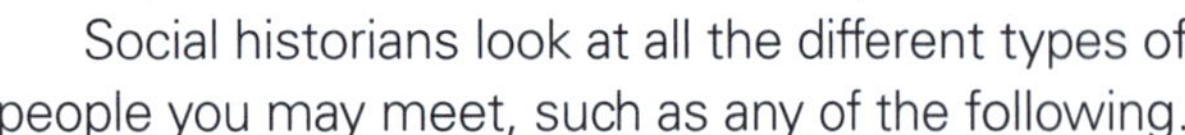

TYPES OF PEOPLE			
	artists	bakers	c
	drain diggers	e	fast-food workers
	gardeners	h	i
	jobless	kiwifruit pickers	labourers
	miners	n	o
	PlayStation fans	q	r
	solo parents	teachers	u
	v	w	x-ray technicians
	yachties	zoo-keepers	

The number of social history topics is huge. This is because social history looks at every feature of day-to-day life, such as any of the following.

SOCIAL HISTORY TOPICS					
	architecture	bungy-jumping	clothes	dancing	entertainment
	families	games	holidays	igloos	jazz
	k	laws	medicines	n	o
	punishment	q	religion	sport	technology
	u	v	w	x	y
	z				

1 Name five people alive today (famous or ordinary) whom you think would make good subjects for a history project.

2 Finish the lists of examples of types of people and social history topics.

3 List 10 topics that you might be interested in researching for a project.

4 In the box, write or draw what *social history* is.

 ISBN 9780170367141

UNIT 8
ORAL HISTORY

oral = spoken (opposite is 'written')

oral history = a person talking about an event or time he or she lived through; recorded on video or tape or paper

Oral histories
- are ordinary people telling others about their lives
- are another way besides reading to learn about the past
- are still used by some cultures to pass on knowledge
- give important historical evidence about people, especially minority groups, who have not featured much in history books
- bring museum displays to life
- are important sources for many radio and TV programs
- can be used in courts as evidence, e.g. land claims
- are from the point of view of the people concerned, e.g. you talking about the day you survived an earthquake
- are used for family histories
- are used in the history of a local community.

Examples: These people have very interesting oral histories to tell of particular events.
- Jai was 10 years old when he came from India with his parents to live in Australia.
- Coreen was 13 when she first saw a non-Aboriginal person.
- Stu was a student in 1969 when the whole school listened on the radio to Neil Armstrong becoming the first person to walk on the moon.

1 Write an event from your life so far that might make an interesting oral history.

____

2 State why oral histories can do the following.

a give older people a sense of worth ______________________________

b make a historical event more exciting to hear about ______________________________

____

3 Name people who might be able to talk to you about the following.

a the day you were born ______________________________

b Australian swimmer Ian Thorpe winning three gold medals at the 2000 Sydney Olympics

____

4 In the box, write or draw what *oral history* is.

ISBN 9780170367141

UNIT 9
MAKING ORAL HISTORY

Check out the topic and questions that you want to answer, e.g. *'What was it like being a teenager in the 1960s?'*

Think of things people can tell you about their first-hand experience of being a teenager in the 1960s, e.g. the music they listened to, and the uniform they wore to school.

Write down 10 questions on the topic that you could use to get information, e.g. *'What was exciting about being a teenager in the 1960s?'*

Use questions that need more than a Yes/No answer, e.g. instead of asking *'Did your family have a car?'*, you could ask *'What forms of transport did your family have?'*

Find someone to interview. The person needs to be old enough to have been a teenager in the 1960s. Relatives? Neighbours? Grandparents?

Phone or visit to introduce yourself. Give your name, age, class and school. Describe your topic. Ask if you can record the conversation. Ask if you can share the information you gather, e.g. write it up for a class report or a project for your teacher to mark.

Good interview manners

1. Be on time.
2. Be ready (questions organised, recording equipment working, spare phone charger).
3. Be polite (e.g. say 'please' and 'thank you').
4. Be respectful (e.g. call the person Mr, Mrs, Miss, Grandpa, Aunt ...).
5. Be patient.
6. Don't argue with or correct the speaker.
7. Listen carefully.
8. Write down any follow-up questions while the speaker is talking so you can ask them during a pause.
9. Thank the person.
10. You might like to send a thank-you note later, or even a copy of your written-up material for the person to keep.

1 Under each sketch, show why the student is being a bad interviewer.

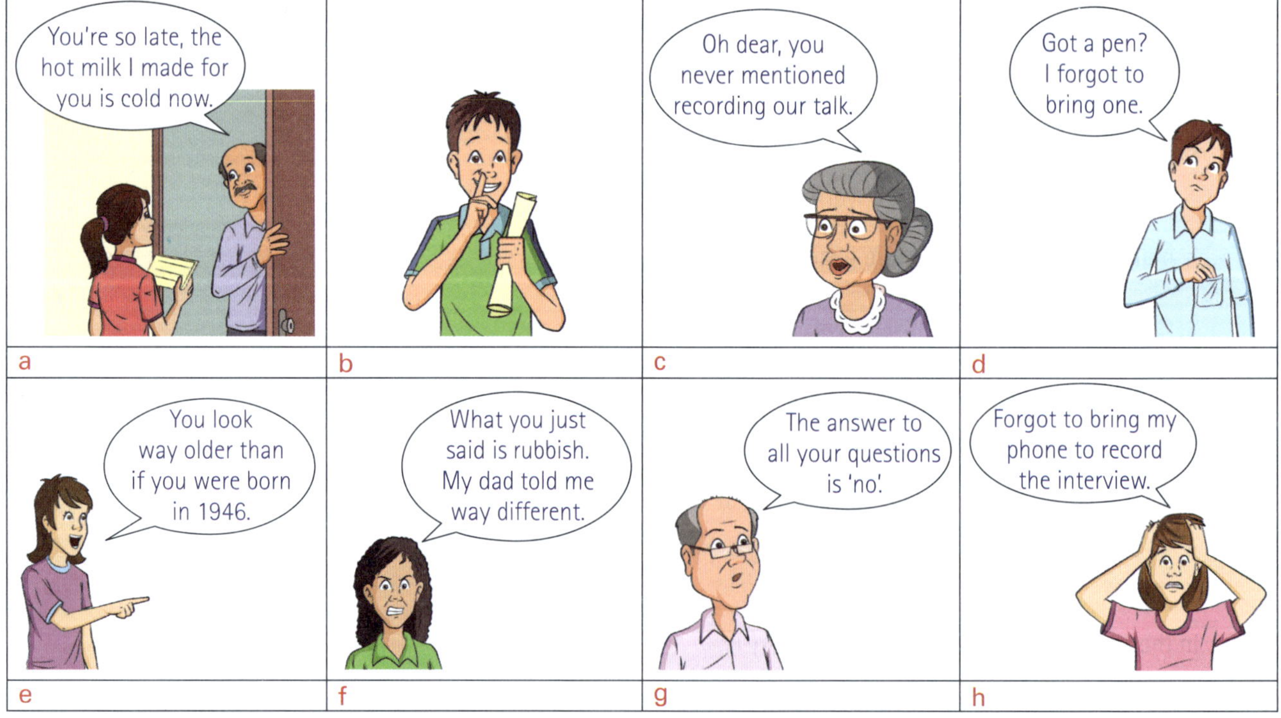

2 In the box, write or draw what *making oral history* is.

ISBN 9780170367141

UNIT 10
A SITE STUDY IN THE LOCAL COMMUNITY

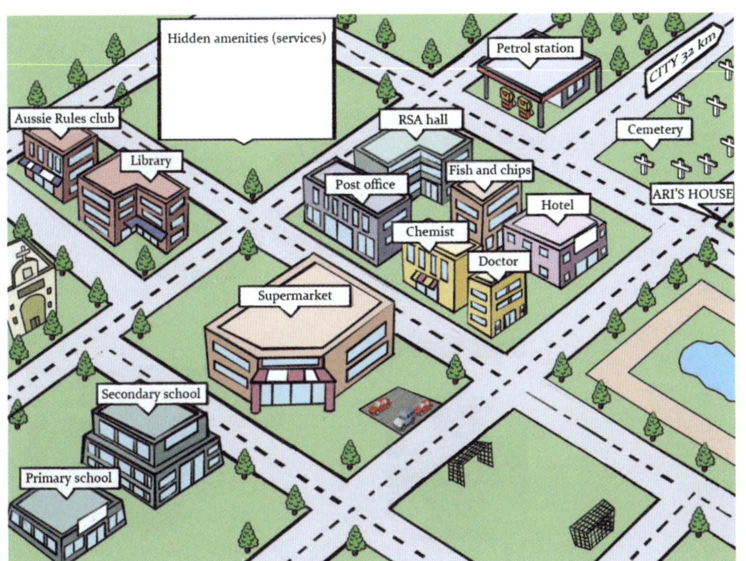

Local is
- from a Latin word meaning *place*
- to do with a small area rather than the whole country or region.

Community is
- from Latin words meaning *common*
- a group of people living in a place.

Local community is
- an area in the countryside, such as a small town, or in a city, such as a suburb
- the area near you where you would go if there was an emergency
- a group of people who live in the same area and interact with each other.

You may be asked to do a special study of an important historic building or construction in your local community. You could choose an old house. Or you could choose a wall of plaques in the local cemetery, or a monument in your local area that commemorates local soldiers who fought in the wars.

Following are some questions to answer to show why your historic building/construction is important:
- What is its function?
- What does it look like?
- Does it have a link to someone important?
- Does it have a link to an important event?

1 In the 'hidden amenities' box in the picture above, list amenities that may also be available to Ari and his family in the local community, e.g. trumpet lessons, night classes or a garden centre in someone's backyard.

2 Either draw or explain how Ari's local community is similar to, or different from, your local community.

3 Historic building or construction

a Name a historic building or construction in your local community on which you could do a special study.

b Why is it an important building? ______

4 In the box, write or draw what a *local community* is.

ISBN 9780170367141

UNIT 11
ARTEFACTS

artefact (also spelt artifact) = an object such as a tool or work of art made by humans, usually from a time before the present; it has a history such as where and when it was made and can tell us a lot about how people lived at a particular time. Archaeologists interpret artefacts.

Examples:

At the Melbourne Museum you can see children's traditional artefacts such as marbles, knucklebones, home-made dried-apple dolls and wire cars.

Some Australian artefacts are so precious they are put on a special list. The list is called the National Cultural Heritage Control List. Some artefacts are listed as Class A. You are not allowed to take Class A artefacts out of Australia.

Examples of Class A artefacts

Victoria Crosses awarded to Australians.

Each piece of the suit of metal armour that Ned Kelly wore at the siege of Glenrowan in Victoria 1880.

Some Aboriginal and Torres Strait Islander artefacts

Bark and log coffins used for traditional burials.

Rock art.

Dendroglyphs (tree carvings).

1 List five objects from your house that a historian in 50 years' time might call artefacts and be excited to see.

2 Suggest one difference between your 'toys' and the traditional ones kept at the Melbourne Museum.

3 Look at the information about the National Cultural Heritage Control List.

a About how old are the Ned Kelly artefacts?

b Why are people given a Victoria Cross?

c Why might someone try to take a Class A artefact out of Australia?

d Give a reason why the special list is called National Cultural Heritage Control. (Clue = the answer is in the name of the list)

ISBN 9780170367141

UNIT 12

PRIMARY AND SECONDARY SOURCES

Primary source:

- comes first, like primary school
- was made during the time or event you are studying
- lets you get as close as possible to what actually happened.

Examples:

A globe made in England in 1890 is a primary source (see below left). It was made more than 125 years ago. But a drawing of the globe (as seen below right), which you made in 2015, is a secondary source because you were not alive in England in 1890.

A speech given by a Senator at the National Museum of Australia in 2004 about the return of Aboriginal artefacts from Sweden to Australia is a primary source because the speaker was involved in the event. But a book about the return of the artefacts written by you in 2018 is a secondary source because you were not involved in the event.

Secondary source:

- comes later, like secondary school
- was made during the present or at a time later than the time or event you are studying
- was made by somebody who was not present at the time or event.

Science & Society Picture Library/Science Museum

A globe made in 1890

A secondary source

1 Future primary sources

a Name an interesting event that is happening in the world at the moment.

____

b Name two primary sources that a historian writing about this event in 20 years' time would find interesting.

____

2 All the sources below are about the Eureka Rebellion on the Ballarat goldfields on 3 December 1854. Put P (for primary) or S (for secondary) beside each of the following to show what type of source it is.

- ☐ Sketch, titled *Slaughter*, dated 3 December 1854, from the sketchbook of Charles Doudiet
- ☐ Book titled *Eureka* by John Molony, published in 1984
- ☐ Poster announcing a meeting of miners on Bakery Hill in 1854
- ☐ Report in *The Argus* of 5 December 1854 about the Eureka Stockade rebellion
- ☐ Memorial stone placed at the Eureka Monument in 1886
- ☐ Film called *Eureka Stockade*, made in 1949
- ☐ Book called *The Eureka Stockade* (1855) by Raffaello Carboni, an eyewitness account by a participant
- ☐ Entry in *Electronic Encyclopedia of Gold in Australia* in 2014 about the Eureka Stockade
- ☐ The Eureka flag that was flown at Bakery Hill in 1854 by the rebel miners who swore an oath to the flag
- ☐ A letter written on 4 December 1854 by a young Englishman living in Ballarat supporting the miners

3 In the box, write what the difference is between *primary and secondary sources*.

ISBN 9780170367141

UNIT 13

USING THE INTERNET FOR HISTORY RESEARCH

> **Internet** = worldwide computer network
>
> **research** = careful search for information

Finding websites on the Internet

- Many historical societies, university libraries and state archives have history resources available online. Ask your local historical organisations if they have lists of websites.
- Ask your teacher or librarian to recommend websites.
- Use your library catalogue to check published guides to websites. Search for 'History – Computer network resources'. But remember, websites can change or disappear.
- Use subject directories to show you a wide choice of resources on your topic, e.g. the World Wide Web Virtual Library: History [http://vlib.iue.it].

Using a search engine

- A popular search engine is Google [www.google.com.au].
- Break your topic into ideas, e.g. if you want information on the 1946 strike over land and pay rights by West Australian Aboriginal stock and sheep workers on De Grey station in the Pilbara, your ideas will be: 1946, Pilbara, strike.
- List key words to describe ideas. Some ideas may have only one key word. Some may have many, e.g. 1946; Pilbara, station; strike, Aboriginal, stock, sheep, workers, pay, land, rights.
- Sort out how your key words fit together. This is called Boolean logic. It lets you show relationships among key words (search terms) by using 'and' logic, 'or' logic, 'not' logic.
- Use 'not' to keep out material you do not want.
- Use synonyms (words that mean the same) or alternative spellings in your search. Connect them with 'or'.
- Some search engines use Boolean logic but use other words instead of 'and', 'or', 'not', e.g. listing search terms and choosing that 'all' terms be searched is 'and' logic; choosing 'any' terms is 'or' logic; using the + symbol is 'and' logic.
- If a search term is more than one word, put it in quotations, e.g. 'sheep workers'.
- You may need to repeat your search a few times using search terms in different combinations until you get good results.
- Ensure your spelling is correct.
- Experiment with different search engines.

Finding historic images

- Check a major collection of photographs, e.g. Trove by the National Library of Australia, the Australian War Memorial or a commercial photo library such as Getty Images.
- Use a search engine for a topic search such as 'Australian heroes' to find photos, drawings or reproductions of paintings.
- Check the 'images' option in Google.

1 Underline or highlight words in the unit that you think will help you become an expert Internet researcher.

2 In the box, write a summary of your underlined or highlighted words.

ISBN 9780170367141

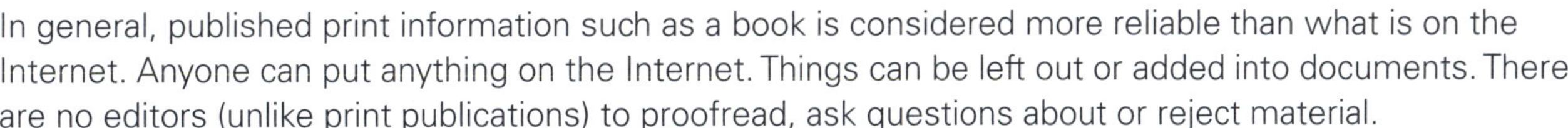

UNIT 14
HOW TO EVALUATE HISTORY WEBSITES

In general, published print information such as a book is considered more reliable than what is on the Internet. Anyone can put anything on the Internet. Things can be left out or added into documents. There are no editors (unlike print publications) to proofread, ask questions about or reject material.

But many publishers and organisations such as governments make wonderful material available by putting it on the Internet.

As a researcher, you have to be able to sort out the reliable from the rubbish.

Check the URLs

Many URLs (Uniform Resource Locator or website address) include the name and type of organisation responsible. The three-letter domain codes give hints about the organisation.

Examples:

.edu = educational institution

.gov = government website

.org = organisation or association

.com = commercial website

.museum = museum

.net = personal or other website

Generally, educational or government websites are more reliable than personal websites.

Check for an author

Who is the author or organisation? What qualifications do they have? Is there a contact address? Is there an 'about' link that gives information about them? No author or organisation named means the information may not be reliable.

Check for the aim of the website

To inform? To sell something? To give opinions? To insist you believe something? If the aim is to do other than inform, you need to examine material carefully before accepting it as fact.

Check to see if the website is reviewed

Look up the website in history subject directories.

Check the website design

Can you read the material easily? Are explanations clear? Are there navigational aids that give access to documents? Are there links to the homepage? Do the links work? Is the information stale? (Never use undated factual or statistical information.) Generally, good design is a sign that material has come from, and is being looked after, by a reliable source.

Check for fairness

Clues to fairness = Balanced, reasoned argument. Accurate outline of ideas or claims made by opponents. Calm, reasoned tone. Material presented without trying to get you emotionally steamed up. Dates given for when material was written. Good grammar and spelling.

Clues to unfairness = Slang or casual language (e.g. Opponents of the Aussies were drongos). Exaggeration (e.g. Thousands of children were stolen every day in Australia). Sweeping statements (e.g. That Australian prime minister was the worst ever). Conflict of interest (e.g. Our competitor's history websites are trash). Angry, mean, critical tone (e.g. Would you, as a sensible Australian, trust THAT man?). One-sided view (e.g. There is only one possible interpretation of the reason Australia signed a treaty with Indonesia).

1 Underline or highlight words that will help make you an expert at evaluating historical websites.

2 In the box, write a summary of your underlined or highlighted words.

UNIT 15

MULTICHOICE QUESTIONS

Multichoice questions can test how well you interpret or understand sources by offering you a choice of answers. You have to choose the best answer and show your choice with a tick or circle.

Example:
The countries shown as fish are
- a) Japan and Indonesia
- b) Papua New Guinea and Timor
- ✓c) Australia and New Zealand

The clue is the shape of the countries. The big fish is shaped like Australia and the little fish is shaped like New Zealand. This means that a) and b) are wrong.

After the big fish has gobbled the small fish, the big fish shows
- a) sadness
- ✓b) happiness
- c) no emotion

The big fish looks like 'the cat that ate the cream'. Its expression shows it is very pleased with itself, is satisfied and full. So the only possible answer is b).

1 Look at the following table from Australian history and answer the two questions about it.

UNEMPLOYMENT RATES IN AUSTRALIA 1928–1936

Year	Unemployment	% of population
1928	45 669	10.8
1929	45 359	11.1
1930	84 767	19.3
1931	117 866	27.4
1932	120 454	29.0
1933	104 035	25.1
1934	86 866	20.5
1935	71 823	16.5
1936	53 992	12.2

QUESTION 1

If the unemployment rate continued in the direction it was going after 1936, the figure for 1937 would be

- A higher than that for 1934.
- B lower than that for 1930.
- C about the same as that for 1936.

QUESTION 2

Which one of the following statements is correct?

- A Unemployment hit a high in 1932.
- B By 1936 unemployment had been falling for six years.
- C Less than a quarter of the population had been unemployed at any one year.

2 In the box, write how to answer *multichoice questions*.

 ISBN 9780170367141

UNIT 16
SHORT ANSWER QUESTIONS

Short answer questions can test how well you interpret or understand sources by asking you questions that have only one correct answer.

Example:

On 25 April 1915, Australian and New Zealand soldiers landed on the Gallipoli Peninsula to fight the Turks.

1. What is the name of the body of water to the east of the Gallipoli Peninsula? *(Dardanelles)*
2. What is the most southern point named on the map? *(Cape Helles)*
3. Which name on the map is the one most likely to have been added after the Gallipoli campaign, and why? *(Anzac Cove, because it would not have been called that before the Anzac soldiers landed there to fight the Turks)*

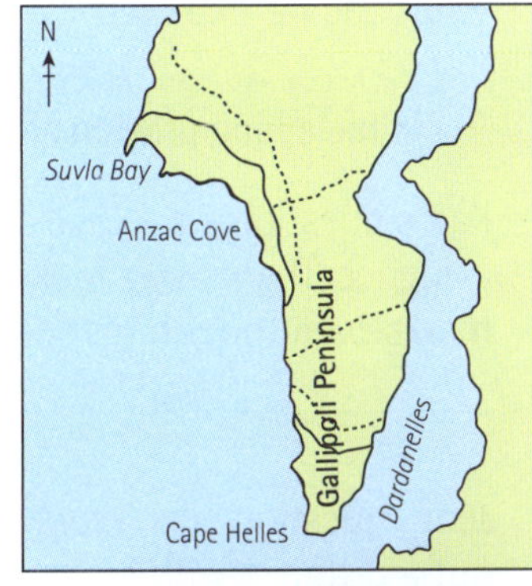

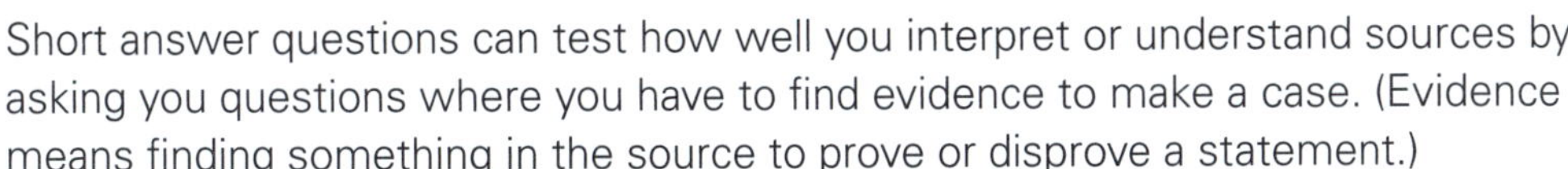

Short answer questions can test how well you interpret or understand sources by asking you questions where you have to find evidence to make a case. (Evidence means finding something in the source to prove or disprove a statement.)

Corbis/Kirn Vintage Stock

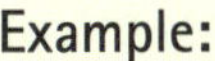

Example:

Give one piece of evidence to show this photo comes from an earlier time than the present.

(example answer) The clothes suggest the picture comes from the late nineteenth century. The girl wears frills, a bow, stockings and a high-necked, long-sleeved pinafore-style dress; the boy wears a button-up jacket and a large bow tie. These clothes were what middle-class or upper-class children of that time wore.

1 Look carefully at the cartoon and answer the questions about it.

a What date was the cartoon published?

____

b What does the box in the cartoon represent?

____

c What sport does the cartoonist use to deliver his message?

____

d Give a historical reason why the cartoonist used this particular sport.

____

e What does the cartoonist suggest is the likely outcome of the election?

____

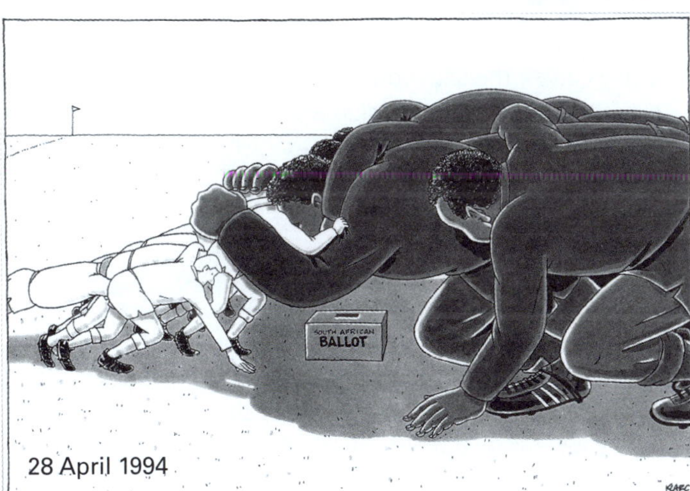

In the 1990s, South Africa's policy of apartheid, which had kept whites in charge and blacks not allowed to vote, was removed.

2 In the box, write how to answer *short answer* questions.

UNIT 17
ANSWERING THE QUESTION

Answering the question means just that – answering the question that you are given. To do that, all you have to do is READ the question, and then ANSWER it. Don't include everything you know about the topic, just what has been asked. One of the skills you are being tested on is how well you can follow directions.

1 In the space provided in each box below, write what each student should have done to get a better mark.

Kasi's question was *'Give one piece of evidence that shows ....'* Kasi spent a lot of time giving two pieces of evidence. The marker looked only at the first piece of evidence that Kasi gave. Kasi got that wrong. Kasi scored no marks even though his second answer was correct.

Jeni's question was *'Work out the approximate distance Alexander's army travelled.'* Jeni wasted time by working out a distance with several decimal points in it. Jeni scored no extra marks and had to rush the rest of the question.

Von's question was *'Refer to Source B'.* Von decided to use Source A instead even though she had just answered a question about Source A. Von scored no marks for her answer.

Adoni's question was *'Quote the sentence from the first paragraph that is most likely to be an opinion.'* Adoni found the sentence. It was long. He rewrote it in his own words. He got the answer wrong because he did not quote it.

Di was given the same question as Adoni. Di quoted the first six words and the last six words of the sentence exactly. She left out the middle six words. To show she had left the six words out she used an ellipsis (...). Di got the answer right.

Raz was asked to write an essay of 300–400 words. Raz loved the essay topic. He wrote 2000 words. The marker put a line through the last 1600 words to show they had not been read.

Jac was asked to write an essay about why the policy of apartheid began in South Africa. Jac did not like the idea of apartheid. Most of her essay was about how bad apartheid was rather than why it was introduced. She scored a very low mark.

Sanjay was asked to imagine he was the prime minister and to give a speech about Australia's nuclear policy. Sanjay was a fan of the PM. He listed all the great things, in his opinion, that the PM had done in welfare, education, health and trade. He mentioned the nuclear policy only briefly. Sanjay scored a low mark.

2 In the box, write what *answering the question* means and why you need to do it.

ISBN 9780170367141

UNIT 18
EDITING YOUR WRITING

To make sure you have prepared your material in the best possible way, therefore qualifying you for excellent grades, you need to check or edit your writing.

Read the topic carefully. Do what it tells you to do, e.g. describe, give reasons for, analyse the results of, imagine you are, explain.

Write on the topic only, e.g. you may know a lot about Australia's nuclear policy, but if the topic is the anti-nuclear policy of the 1970s, write about the 1970s and NOT before and after.

Be clear, e.g. 'Hitler walked into prison and began to write the book *Mein Kampf*.'

Avoid writing silly sentences, e.g. Walking into prison, Hitler wrote the book *Mein Kampf*. (How can you write a book as you walk into prison?)

Use short sentences with capital letters and full stops, e.g. 'In 1986, the Commonwealth Heads of Government met in London.'

Avoid using 'etc.' because it suggests you have run out of ideas.

Be tidy. If the marker cannot read your work, the marker cannot grade it.

Cross out mistakes, rather than using white-out.

Watch spelling, e.g. 'There lay the Pasific Ocean, their armies lost.' (Pasific is spelt incorrectly.)

Keep tenses all the same, e.g. 'In 1941 Japanese bombers *sank* the two British ships defending Singapore. In 1942 Singapore *surrendered* to Japan.' OR 'In 1941 Japanese bombers *sink* the two British ships defending Singapore. In 1942 Singapore *surrenders* to Japan.'

Watch apostrophes, e.g. Lord's lady = one lord, one lady; lord's ladies = one lord, more than one lady; lords' lady = more than one lord, one lady; lords' ladies = more than one lord, more than one lady. (You can avoid apostrophes by using the word 'of', e.g. the lady of the lord.)

Avoid contractions (e.g. couldn't, didn't) unless you are writing direct speech.

Watch 'its' and 'it's', e.g. 'Italy swallowed its pride and surrendered; 'It's a nice day,' the Archduke was probably saying.'

Avoid abbreviations, especially the first time you use the word/s.

Use capitals for titles and places, e.g. The Prime Minister of Australia; The Timor Gap Treaty between Australia and Indonesia.

Check what you have written. In an exam, read it silently. Outside an exam, read it aloud.

Frontispiece of 'Mein-Kampf' by Adolf Hitler (1889-1945), c.1938 (litho), German School, (20th century), Bridgeman Images/Archives Charmet/Private Collection

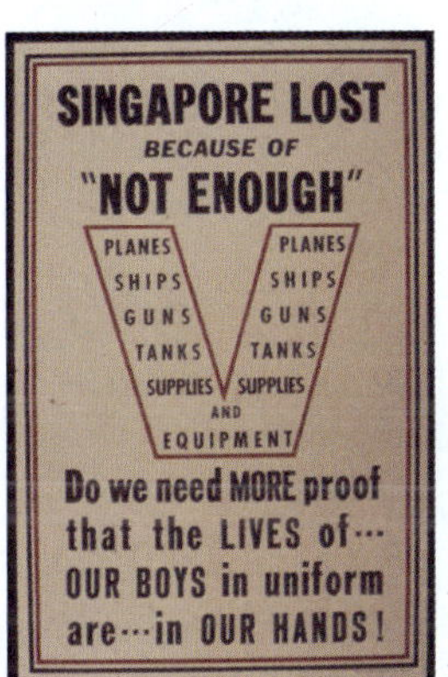

Alamy/war posters

1 The facts below are correct but there are about 30 sloppy mistakes. Circle them.

The treaty of versailles 1919 after WW1 p the Krauts off, this was Especially as they have no reps at the conference which organised the treaty. Led by president wilson of the USA, the leaders set up a kind of international club called the league of nations to keep the piece and stop wars for ever they decided that Germany was responsibilty for ww1 & must be punished for causing so much damage. Gm is ordered to pay lotsa dough. Gm lost it's kolonys as they was given to other countrys. Forbid to have submarines, military aeroplanes etc.

2 In the box, write why it is important to *edit your writing.*

ISBN 9780170367141

UNIT 19
WRITING A PARAGRAPH

paragraph = group of sentences with a common topic; starts a new line on a page

Example:

G = Generalisation – introductory sentence about the topic of the paragraph

E = Explanation – explains more about the topic

E = Example – something that illustrates the explanation

D = Diagram – graphic about the topic to give visual information (not always needed)

In 1950, communist North Korea invaded non-communist South Korea. The United Nations asked North Korea to leave South Korea. When this did not happen, the United Nations gathered an army to defend South Korea. Australia, which was concerned that communism was starting to spread through Asia, joined 15 other countries in a war in Korea against the communists.

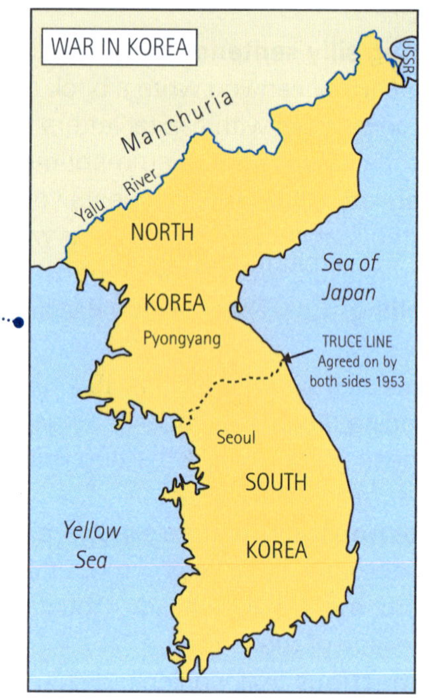

1 For each GEED, circle the letter that the meaning refers to.

a G E E D the optional one

b G E E D the sentence stating the topic

c G E E D the illustration of the explanation

d G E E D the explanation of the topic

2 Show the correct order of the following sentences for a paragraph by putting a, b and c beside the GEE.

G E E

a She read a lot of Greek and Latin, was good at French and Italian, and later also learnt Spanish.

b With the help of her tutors, Elizabeth became an excellent student.

c As a child, Queen Elizabeth I seldom lived in one place for long but her education did not suffer.

3 In the box, write what a *paragraph* is.

ISBN 9780170367141

UNIT 20
QUOTATION

Example:
'The historian is a sort of talking ghost from out of the past.' (Ernst Hoffman)

quotation = a piece of writing taken directly from a person or book, using the person's or book's own words, rather than your own words

Rules for how to show quotations in your paragraph or essay

1. Put the quotation inside quotation marks. Quotation marks are also called *inverted commas*.
2. Use single quotation marks.
3. Put the full stop or comma that ends the quotation inside the quotation mark.
4. Use double quotation marks to show a quotation within the quotation.
5. If you use only part of the quotation, use three dots (called an *ellipsis*) to show that you have missed out words.
6. Long quotations are called block quotations. Indent them on both margins.
7. Short quotes of two lines or less can go in the text.
8. Put anything you add to a quote inside square brackets.
9. If the quotation has a mistake in it and you want to show that the mistake is in the original and is not your mistake, put the word 'sic' in brackets ('sic' is a Latin word meaning 'thus it was written').
10. Avoid using long quotations because readers tend to skip over them.

My essay seeks to show that leaders have had different attitudes to war. Julius Caesar made his ideas plain when he said 'Veni, vidi, vici.' [I came, I saw, I conquered.] American President Theodore Roosevelt was more cautious when he said in a famous speech of 1901, 'There is a homely adage which runs: "Speak softly and carry a big stick: you will go far."' The great British war-time leader Winston Churchill gave many rousing speeches about the war, declaring '… we shall fight on the beaches, we shall fight on the landing grounds … we shall never surrender…' And William Tecumseh Sherman gave a passionate speech in 1880, saying

> *'There is many a boy here today who looks on war as all glory, but, boys, it is all hell. You can bear this warning voice to generations yet to come. I look upon war with horror.'*

One famous historian, writing on this topic, used a quotation from British Prime Minister Margaret Thatcher, 'We fought to show that aggression does not pay and that the robber cannot be allowed to get away with his swag.'

1 In the box, write a quotation for which you would like to be remembered. Put it inside quotation marks and put your name in brackets at the end.

2 Draw arrows from rules 1–8 (above) to examples in the essay beside them.

3 In the box, write what a *quotation* is.

UNIT 21
ESSAY STRUCTURE

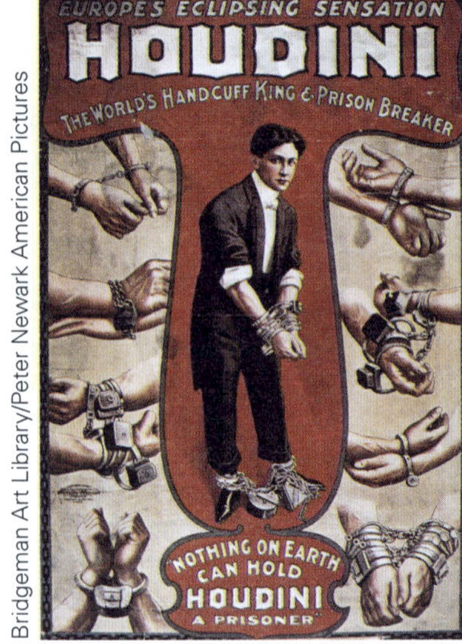

Bridgeman Art Library/Peter Newark American Pictures

Example:

An essay on Harry Houdini (a stunt performer) might be two pages long and talk about his real name (Ehrich Weiss), his nickname (The Handcuff King), his skills (physical fitness and self-control), his escape from everything he was locked up in (e.g. straitjacket, sunken packing crate, padded cell, coffin, diving suit, plate glass box, padlocks) and his famous saying ('My brain is the key that sets me free').

essay = short piece of non-fiction writing about a particular subject

structure = how it is made. A house's structure is how it was designed and built; an essay's structure is how it was designed and written.

Reasons for having a structure for your essay:

- it is easy to write
- it is easy to read
- it is easy to mark.

head = introduction, what essay is about

body = several paragraphs, each paragraph is about a different point

tail = summary, sums up, no new information, just summary of main points

Example:

What was the Great Hunger and what results did it have for Ireland? — Essay topic

The Great Hunger occurred in Ireland from 1845 to 1849. It was also called The Great Famine. The potato was the most important food in Ireland. But for several harvests, a fungus attacked potatoes. This had serious results for Ireland. — Head

Most families depended on potatoes for their food. Most Irish farmers relied on the potato harvest for their money. The fungus made potatoes go bad. Many Irish had nothing to eat but rotten potatoes. About a million people died of starvation. Many others died of diseases to do with famine – cholera, dysentery, typhus. When corpses were left to rot, rats and other animals ate them.

The British Government, which was responsible for ruling Ireland at this time, made a few efforts to help, such as opening relief centres. But much of the British public did not approve of even this little help. They thought the Irish were lazy and did not deserve hand-outs.

A quarter of Ireland's population fled. They went mainly to North America, Australia and New Zealand. But they never forgot their culture.

The Irish believed the British had betrayed them. They said it was time for the Irish to control their own affairs. Some said the Irish should take up arms against the British to get them out of Ireland. — Body

The Ireland at the beginning of the Great Hunger was different from the Ireland at the end of it. Many people had died of starvation and disease. Many others had fled to other countries. Ireland was left with survivors whose attitudes towards the British had hardened. — Tail

ISBN 9780170367141

1 Give two reasons why the Harry Potter books are NOT called essays.

a ______________________ b ______________________

2 Give three reasons why you should follow a set structure when you write an essay.

____

____

3 In the box, draw the outline of the head, body and tail of your favourite animal. In each body part, add a few words that will help you remember how to structure an essay.

4 Read the essay in this unit and tick each point that the writer has made. Give it a grade: 9 or more ticks = A, 7–8 ticks = B, 5–6 ticks = C, below 5 = D. In the second box, put a reason why the essay writer was given 10 out of 10 for the STRUCTURE of the essay.

GRADE	

5 In the box, write or draw how to *structure an essay*.

ISBN 9780170367141

UNIT 22
BIBLIOGRAPHY

How to set out items in a bibliography

> **bibliography** = a list of books or other material, such as magazines, newspapers, DVDs, interviews, podcasts and the Internet, that you used to help you write your essay; it is written in alphabetical order using the surnames of authors and appears at the end of your essay

- Arrange the items in order of author surnames alphabetically.
- Give the name of the author/s (surname, first names or initials), e.g. Bones, H.
- Give the title (it may be underlined if you are writing by hand, or put in italics if printed), capitalise the first word of the title and other important words (except for small words such as *of, and, in, an, a*), e.g. The History of Rap Music or *The History of Rap Music*.
- Give the place of publication (use only the name of cities or towns), e.g. New York.
- Give the publisher and shorten the publisher's name, e.g. Hooper (not the whole name of Hooper Publishing Co., Inc.).
- Give the year of publication (NOT the date of printing such as '4th printing 2015'), e.g. 2015.
- Give the page numbers for articles from magazines, encyclopedias, journals and so on; but they are not needed for a book.

Example: King, John, *The Wonderful History of Australia*, Melbourne, Kanga Press, 2015.

You need to use a bibliography:

- to show the sources of your ideas, quotations, diagrams and so on
- to show you are respectful of other people's work and are not stealing it and trying to pass it off as your own original work (plagiarism)
- to give extra information to readers who might like to use your sources to do more reading on the topic
- to let the reader check your sources to see if they, and you, are correct.

1 What piece of information is missing from each of the following?

a Taylor, Jess, *A Skateboarder's History of the World*, 2005, Gentry Press ____________

b Locke, Billy, *The History of the Simpsons*, Boston, 2003 ____________

c Knopp, Guido, *Hitler's Children*, Sutton Publishing Ltd, 2002 ____________

2 Give the main reason you will always use a bibliography for your essay.

____

3 In the box, write what a *bibliography* is.

ISBN 9780170367141

UNIT 23
GLOSSARY

Example:

Alliance formal agreement between two people or countries
Anti-semitism dislike of Jews
Apartheid policy in South Africa to separate races; ended in 1991
Armistice agreement to put a temporary stop to fighting
Boycott to avoid buying from a company or country as a protest
Citizen member of a particular community or country
Coup d'état overthrow of a government by force
Exile being forced to leave native land
Guerrilla warfare surprise hit-and-run attacks by small, fast units
Hierarchy persons or things arranged in order of rank
indigenous native to a place
Nationalisation transferring ownership (e.g. of railway) to the state
Peasant having more than one wife or husband at the same time
Polygamy small farmer or farm worker
Urbanisation development of towns and cities
Reform change
Terrorism using acts or threats of violence, especially as a political weapon

glossary = a list of technical or unusual words used in a book, along with their meanings; it is written in alphabetical order and normally appears at the end of the book

1 Write down four things you notice about how the glossary is set out.

a ____________________ b ____________________

c ____________________ d ____________________

2 There are three deliberate mistakes in the glossary above. Highlight or circle them.

3 Add the following six terms to the glossary to show where they should go.

Balance of power, Minority, Standard of living, Ethnic group, Revolution, Fascism

4 Give two entries for a glossary, along with their meanings, you would use if you wrote a book about your favourite sport, pastime or music.

____

____

5 In the box, write or draw what a *glossary* is.

ISBN 9780170367141

UNIT 24

BEING SCEPTICAL (A CRITICAL ANALYSIS)

Example: The following was posted on the Internet as a happy story.

A poor Scottish farmer called Fleming saved a young boy called Winston from drowning. Winston's father was so grateful that he paid for Fleming's son to be educated and become the doctor he had always dreamt of being. Fleming's son became Sir Alexander Fleming, famous discoverer of penicillin. Winston became Sir Winston Churchill, famous British prime minister. When Winston lay ill with pneumonia, penicillin saved his life.

sceptical = unwilling to believe something without questioning or checking to see if it is true (comes from the Greek *skeptikos*, which means 'thoughtful')

Many people accepted the story as true and it was repeated around the world. However, people who were more sceptical pointed out the following:

- There are many different versions of this story. In one version, it was Alexander, not his father, who saved Winston from drowning.
- Winston was seven years older than Alexander so Alexander would have been too small to rescue Winston from drowning.
- No biography about Churchill mentions Winston's meeting with the Flemings.
- The Flemings lived in an isolated part of Scotland; Winston was unlikely to be on holiday there.
- Alexander did not leave the farm to race off to medical school; he did other jobs before deciding to go.
- Alexander's medical school education was paid for by an inheritance from an uncle.
- Winston Churchill did get sick with what was probably pneumonia but was treated with sulphonamide and digitalis (not penicillin).

Alamy/David Cole

All sources have to be questioned or critically analysed. Questions such as, 'Who wrote this document?', 'Why did they write it?', 'Who was the audience?', 'Who benefited?', 'Who doesn't?' should be asked.

1 Think about the Fleming/Churchill story and suggest reasons for the following.

a Why somebody wrote it. ______________________

b Why many people believed it. ______________________

2 Evie read that the Nazis killed 96 million Jews. Josh read that the Nazis killed 6 million Jews. Bella read that the Nazis killed no Jews. Chas read that the Nazis killed 6 million Jews.

a Circle the students who should be the most sceptical.

b Suggest a way the students could find out which figure was right.

____

3 In the box, write what *being sceptical* means.

 ISBN 9780170367141

UNIT 25
EVIDENCE

evidence = facts or information that proves or disproves a belief or proposition

Example:
When Miss Litt accused Cal of wasting time, Cal showed her all the up-to-date work in his History folder as evidence to prove how hard he had been working.

You can collect and present evidence. For example, Mary found a copy of her grandfather's birth certificate, which she used as evidence to prove that he was born in Switzerland.

You can examine a source to find evidence to prove a statement. For example, Saba found evidence in a table of trade figures that gold was an important export in the 1850s for Australia.

You can use any historical resource as evidence. Some examples are:

- Jiro collected photocopies of three cartoons about the 1971 Springbok rugby tour of Australia as evidence of how it caused a state of emergency in Queensland.
- Assi collected 10 newspaper clippings about the earthquake and tsunami that struck Japan in 2011 as evidence for how much overseas aid Australia gave to the surviving victims.
- Meg collected a copy of the original plans for her local community as evidence of how much the town had changed.
- Raul collected a photocopy of a newspaper story about how a 1990 US survey found that Melbourne was the world's best city in which to live. He knew a single piece of evidence needed backing up, so he looked for a copy of the survey to use as further evidence.
- Jan took notes from a website to use as evidence about how the wool industry and gold rushes of the 1850s encouraged settlers to come to Australia. She downloaded an article from another website and highlighted the pieces of evidence in the article.

1 Name a time when you or someone else have offered evidence to prove a point.

2 Name four types of resources that you might be able to use as evidence about the Snowy Mountains Scheme in Australia between 1949 and 1974.

3 In the box, write what *evidence* is.

ISBN 9780170367141

UNIT 26
ORAL EVIDENCE

If you are presenting oral evidence, you do not have to be a great speaker. You just have to speak clearly so people can hear you. If you are presenting evidence that was recorded by someone else, such as a speech from a radio, and the voice is scratchy or hard to hear in places, you could make a paper copy (a transcript) to go with it.

Some examples of giving oral evidence are:

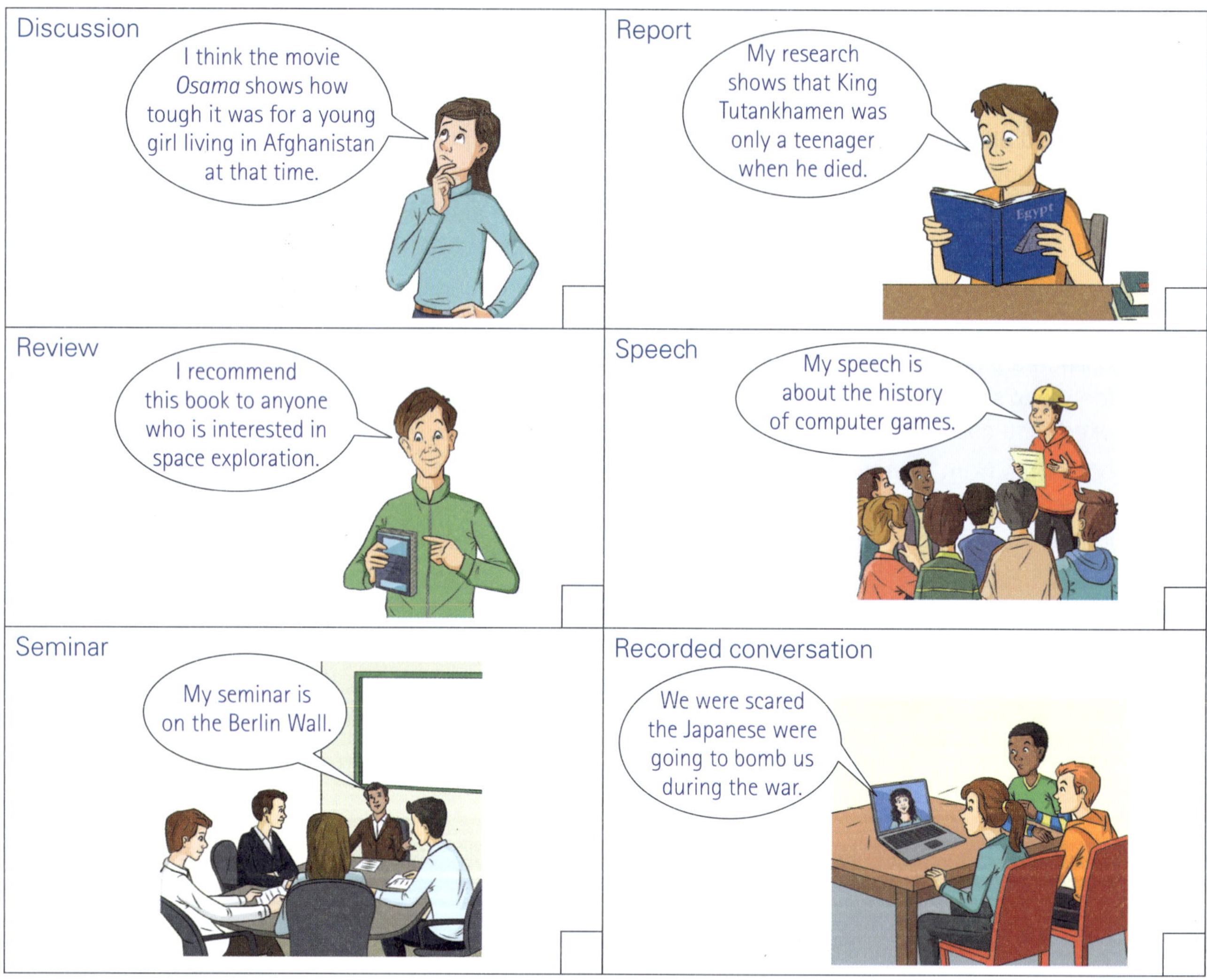

1 In the small boxes above, put the numbers of the descriptions that best suit.

Descriptions: [1] a spoken address, prepared or impromptu (unprepared); [2] giving an account of a particular subject; [3] a class or group talking together to swap opinions about a topic; [4] a recorded talk between the interviewer and person being interviewed; [5] a short, critical talk about something such as a book, film or play; [6] a group of students talking with their teacher for advanced study or research.

2 Give another way of presenting oral evidence.

3 In the box, write or draw what *oral evidence* means.

ISBN 9780170367141

UNIT 27
WRITTEN EVIDENCE

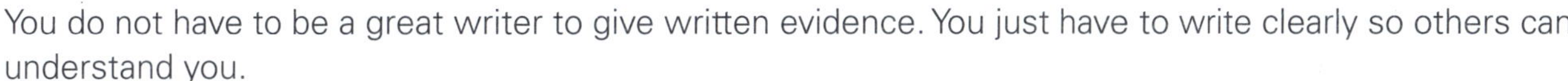

You do not have to be a great writer to give written evidence. You just have to write clearly so others can understand you.

One way you may be asked to give written evidence is through answering questions.

Examples:

Short answer questions	Multichoice questions	Essay

When you are collecting evidence to help you work on a topic, you can use anything written.

Examples:

Diary	Report	Letter	Newspaper
Logbook = record of progress	**Journal** = daily record	Website	

1 Give written evidence by reading the following and writing the answers.

The Mountain Men of the American Wild West were said to have white bodies but the minds of American Indians. Blackfoot Indians once chased Mountain Man John Colter, a trapper, for a week. Completely naked, John ran more than 250 kilometres. When he reached a fort, he was almost dead from hunger and thirst, and he was badly injured. He recovered quickly and went back to the mountains to trap.

Answer each of the following questions with either 'Indian/s' or 'white/s'.

a What colour was John? ______________

b Who were the Blackfoot? ______________

c What colour were Mountain Men? ______________

d Who owned the fort? ______________

2 Give five examples of written evidence. A letter is an example.

____

3 What is

a a difference between a logbook and a journal? ______________

b the main difference between written and oral evidence? ______________

4 In the box, write or draw what *written evidence* is.

ISBN 9780170367141

UNIT 28
PERFORMANCE EVIDENCE

performance = acting, singing, miming, showing or dancing in front of an audience

You do not have to be a great actor to give performance evidence. You just have to speak clearly and/or be aware of body language.

Examples:

video = projected onto a wall or screen

role play = pretending to be someone else to show that person's opinions or actions

practical demonstration = showing how to do something

multimedia presentation = slide show

drama production = a play, usually longer than a role play or sketch and can be live or on video

mime = acting without words

sketch = a short play, often comical

1 Decide which example you would use if you wanted to show the following.

a How early Australian settlers made aprons from sacking. ______

b An argument between a man and woman about women getting the vote, which ends with a chase involving an umbrella. ______

c The end of petrol rationing in Australia in 1950. ______

d A day in the life of a school student in 1900. ______

2 Give another way of presenting performance evidence.

______

3 In the box, write or draw how to give *performance evidence*.

ISBN 9780170367141

UNIT 29
VISUAL EVIDENCE

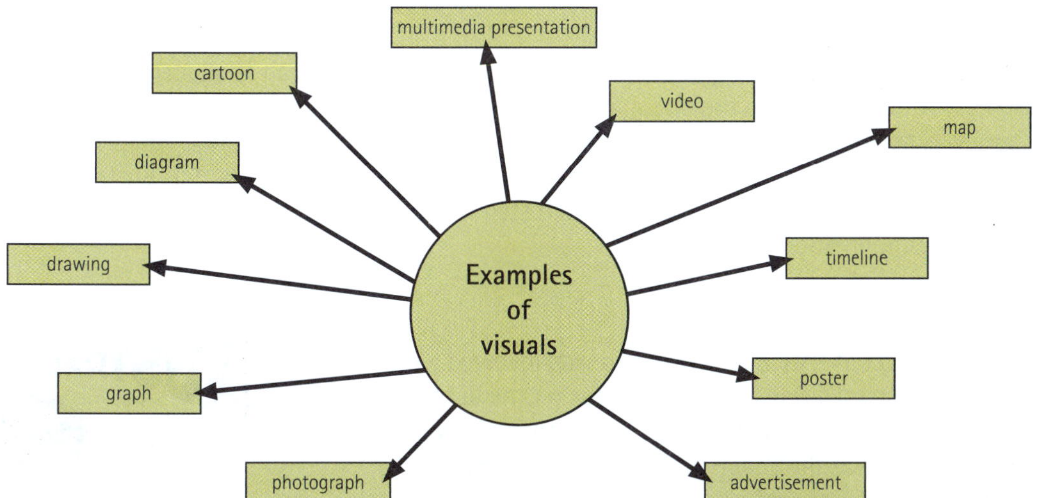

visual = something that uses your sense of sight to help you understand and learn; it is about viewing and visualising, illustrating and illuminating, seeing and showing, understanding and uncovering, amplifying and analysing, learning and links

1 Beside each example of a visual, draw or write something that would help a fellow student understand what the visual looks like, and for what it is used.

2 Write down two things the cartoon below shows. ______________________________

Brockie, Bob: "That settles it then - we test our next volcano in Paris!". National Business Review 6 October 1995. Ref: H-451-003. Alexander Turnbull Library, Wellington, New Zealand. http://natlib.govt.nz/records/22313320

3 In the box, write or draw how to give *visual evidence*.

UNIT 30

ANALYSING VISUAL EVIDENCE

analysing = examining in detail to bring out the full meaning

Example:

Taree analysed a document showing the non-Indigenous (non-Aboriginal and Torres Strait Islander) population at the time of Federation in 1901. By examining the document closely and working out what the statistics on the document meant, Taree was able to make four important discoveries. He discovered the non-Indigenous population in 1901 was 3.9 million. Half of these people lived in cities. Three-quarters were born in Australia. Most were of English, Scottish or Irish descent. Taree was so interested in his analysis that he hunted for documents about the Indigenous population in 1901.

Example:

Kei analysed this visual. She worked out that the sailing ship was involved with Australia Day – it was a symbol. Australia Day is held each year on the date of the arrival in Australia of the First Fleet. She was puzzled by the shape in which '1997' appeared until she realised it was the shape of Australia with Tasmania at the bottom. Kei had thought Australia Day was a recent invention. The 1997 date showed her it had been celebrated for more than 18 years.

1 Analyse the visual on the right by answering the questions about it.

a What type of visual is it? ____________________

b Which three words show you what it is about? ____________________

c Which two countries do the two figures represent? ____________________

d How did you find the answer to c? ____________________

Bromhead, Peter, 1933- : "TransTasman trade tight-rope" 22 November 1987. Ref: A-322-105. Alexander Turnbull Library, Wellington, New Zealand. http://natlib.govt.nz/records/23115240

e What are the two figures doing? ____________________

f What is likely to happen if the figure on the left does as the figure on the right suggests? ____________________

g What is the main message of the cartoon? ____________________

h What does the visual suggest about the trade relationship between the two countries? ____________________

2 In the box, write what *analysing visual evidence* means.

ISBN 9780170367141

UNIT 31
FORMAT

format = the look of material such as a book, magazine, leaflet, brochure, pamphlet, newspaper, film; includes features such as shape, size, layout, font

Example: a newspaper story

bold (heavy text)

by-line (name of writer)

headline

map of place where event took place

story laid out in columns

date line (date and location of story)

fact box (boxed text set out in series of facts, often with bullet points)

photograph of brother and sister

breakout quote (given graphic treatment such as bold or italic type)

caption (says what the photo is about)

not much white space left

NOTE: A newspaper story in 1900 would not have used colour, but a story in the year 2015 would have.

1 Draw arrows from the boxes to the examples in the drawing above.

2 In the box, either draw and label or describe the format of a DVD cover.

3 In the box, either draw and label or describe the format of a poster.

4 In the box, write or draw what *format* means.

UNIT 32
STYLE

Style can be formal or informal

Example:

In the presence of an enormous, enthusiastic crowd of people assembled in front of the Parliamentary Library steps, the Governor-General at 10.30 this morning announced that the armistice between the Allies and Germany had been signed.

Example:

Heaps of people mucked around in front of the Parliamentary Library steps this morning and yelled their heads off. Old Man arrives. Yakked on about Britain with its mates like Australia signing a bit of paper to stop war with those mad-as-hell Huns.

style = way of writing or speaking belonging to a particular group of people or to a particular period of time

formal style = no swearing or slang, using proper spelling and grammar, being polite, addressing people by their correct titles, no abbreviations

informal style = using slang, not worrying about being polite or proper, calling people by their nicknames or Christian names, not worrying too much about grammar

Style is also about point of view or voice

First person style uses 'I' and 'we'

Third person style uses 'he', 'she', 'they'

Examples:

They finished their history project early. It gave them time to check for mistakes.

I glowed with pride. My history project had scored an A.

1. Match the styles on page 35 with their speech bubbles by drawing arrows.
2. Match the formal style and the informal style definitions above with their examples by drawing arrows.
3. Match the first-person style and the third-person style above with their examples by drawing arrows.
4. In the box, write what *style* means.

ISBN 9780170367141

Cut yer name across me backbone
Stretch me skin across a drum
Iron me up on Pinchgut Island
From today till Kingdom come
I will eat your Norfolk dumpling
Like a juicy Spanish plum
Even dance the Newgate hornpipe
If ye'll only give me rum.

Had early tucker.
Now in tent. 2 cobbers arguing – hard cases. One tells other he couldn't find grand piano in one-roomed house.

The Australian flag has been raised at the new Mawson Base in Princess Elizabeth Land in Antarctica, making it the world's most southern human settlement.

Those who lose dreaming are lost. Travellers, there are no paths. Paths are made by walking.

This copy of the Court's Reason for Judgement is subject to formal revision prior to publication in the Australian Commonwealth Law Reports.

They just come with white man's law and that. Peg his ground, how much he like, no ask blackfella, with nothing for them. We feel real hurt. Ground all gone.

This collection consists of about 500 items of folklore told to children by adults in Arabic, Croatian, English, Greek, Italian, Macedonian, Serbian, Spanish and Turkish ... The material includes ... such as baby play, ball bouncing, circle games and rhymes, clapping, counting out, lullabies, games, rhymes, poems, songs and stories. There are also two Pitjantjatjara songs and stories.

Information sheet from the Melbourne Museum (Style = gives information, lists, uses facts and factual language, aims to be easily understood by a wide audience, does not use language that could offend anyone, good grammar)

Aboriginal land rights protester (Style = English as spoken rather than written, not concerned with grammar, unusual and colourful expressions, emotional, expressive, aims to communicate strong feelings, use of special words to describe people)

High Court of Australia 1992 Mabo decision (Style = legal language, often understood only by people in legal jobs, very wordy so that there is no room for misunderstanding, serious, no humour, complicated sentences, good grammar)

Newspaper report of 1954 (Style = tries to squeeze as much information into as short a space as possible, concerned with facts and details, makes facts sound dramatic, good grammar, does not use 'I', 'me', 'my')

Aboriginal proverb (Style = makes you think hard about what it could mean, references to special interests such as Dreamtime and nature, emotional, statement of idea or belief, aims to help others)

Convict rum song/folk tune (Style = not too concerned with grammar as many convicts lacked education; colourful language, humour; song has rhythm and beat, rhyme)

Australian soldier's diary, 1942 (Style = may be written as if writer is talking to a mate, simple language, may use abbreviations and symbols, not worried about grammar, sentences short or unfinished, casual, use of slang, use of 'I', 'me', 'my')

ISBN 9780170367141

UNIT 33
APPROPRIATE FORMAT AND STYLE

appropriate = suitable or fitting

Example:

If you were presented to the Governor-General or the Queen, you could wear your dirty jeans and ripped T-shirt. But because it would be a formal occasion with people in dignified clothes, it would be more appropriate if you wore something clean and tidy. By choosing to wear the inappropriate dirty jeans and ripped T-shirt, you are sending the message that you have little or no respect for the occasion or the people there.

Examples of appropriate format and style

PowerPoint presentation for a Year 7 class about the Athenians and the Spartans

This is a complicated topic so you need to keep it as basic and entertaining as you can for your young audience. Examples of appropriate format and style:

- use very simple language
- use special effects, such as music, to make it more interesting
- use bright colours
- use visuals such as cartoons and maps.

A letter to the editor about the first TV broadcasts in Australia, 1956

The introduction of TV was just in time to cover the Olympic Games in Melbourne, so Australians would be excited to see gold medallists such as Dawn Fraser, Betty Cuthbert and Murray Rose. Examples of appropriate format and style:

- use of 'I', 'me', 'my'
- formal writing (no slang, no swearing)
- opinions expressed in a direct and forceful way
- set out as a letter starting with 'Dear Sir' (at that time all editors were male)
- avoid being offensive (mean and nasty) about people.

An audio-visual display about the life of John Curtin (1885–1945), Prime Minister of Australia

Audio means 'material to listen to' and *visuals* means 'material to look at'. Examples of appropriate format and style:

- John Curtin was a respected and loved PM; many people said he went to an early grave to save his country, so the format and style should be in keeping with this
- use sound effects such as music (e.g. songs of the time) and speeches (e.g. Curtin addressing Australia)
- use material such as maps, graphs, cartoons, photographs
- give each visual a commentary (talk), either written or recorded; keep the commentary short and snappy
- make sure visuals are big enough for people to see easily
- give visuals short captions that make people look at them.

ISBN 9780170367141

A Newspapers in Education (NIE) page in a newspaper about the Vietnam War of the 1960s and 1970s

As this is for young students, it has to look great to get them to read it. Examples of appropriate format and style:

- make it brightly coloured and interesting
- put information in as few words as possible, e.g. use bullet points
- use simple words
- use different fonts with different sizes
- use many visuals such as photographs and maps (if you have only black-and-white photographs, you can brighten them up with colourful frames and coloured captions)
- use white space (blank space on the page) to make material stand out on the page
- language can be more informal but not offensive.

A radio broadcast about the end of the Second World War

The radio broadcast has to paint pictures with words and sound effects because at that time people had no TV. Examples of appropriate format and style:

- an exciting introduction
- some comments from experts
- use proper names and titles for people
- music, e.g. Queen's 'We Are The Champions' would be ideal but you could not use it because Queen were not around in 1945
- a dramatic ending.

1 Circle the best answer for the following.

a Appropriate means right for the times / wrong for the times.

b Inappropriate means right for the times / wrong for the times.

c Appropriate means suitable for the event / unsuitable for the event.

d The most appropriate language for a speech to the United Nations by a world leader would be formal / informal.

e The most appropriate music for a taped commentary about a famous nineteenth-century historical figure would be classical / rap.

f The most appropriate captions for a display of artefacts about the history of toys would be long / short.

2 In the box, write what *appropriate format and style* means.

UNIT 34
DOCUMENT ANALYSIS AND EVALUATION

Example:

Your birth certificate gives information about your parents and your birth. This information, in the form of a document, can be used as evidence that you are who you say you are. It is one of the most important documents about you. The material in it is legitimate because it is factual and comes from an official source.

document = written or printed paper giving evidence or information

analysis = the result of your analysing of the document

evaluation = deciding how useful or important or legitimate (real, fair) the document is

Example:

The National Archives of Australia holds key documents that are the foundation of the nation of Australia. They are Australia's 'birth certificates'. The documents are important in your life today. They belong to all Australians because they helped make Australia. Many are the originals. The documents also remind you that your generation is responsible for making more documents that will help make Australia's future. They are legitimate because they are factual and come from an official source.

Example:

Chinese Immigration Act 1855 (Victoria)

IV On arrival in any port of Victoria of any ship having any Immigrants on board before making entry the master shall pay to the Collector or other proper Officer of Customs a rate of ten pounds for every such Immigrant arrived in such ship and no entry shall be deemed to have been legally made or to have any legal effect whatever until such payment shall have been made and if any master neglect so to specify and state in any such list as aforesaid or to pay such rate within the time aforesaid or shall land or permit any such Immigrant to land at any place in Victoria with the intent of evading the payment of any such rate he shall on conviction be liable to a penalty not exceeding twenty pounds for each Immigrant in addition to the amount of such rate.

Analysis of this document:

- 'IV' shows it is an extract from the Act, not the full Act
- the name of the Act includes 'immigration' and refers to the Chinese
- language is legal, e.g. 'aforesaid', 'deemed', 'be liable to'
- style is formal, e.g. no slang, no humour, no shortened words or abbreviations
- uses many nouns (naming words), e.g. entry, effect, payment
- is about restricting the entry of Chinese people into the Colony of Victoria
- sentences are long
- uses conventions of the time, e.g. ten pounds (about $20)
- makes sure it covers every person and thing, e.g. any port, any ship, any master
- shows clearly the person responsible for payment
- shows clearly to whom payment must be made
- shows clearly the penalty for breaking this law
- names the place the law applies to.

Evaluation

This Act made the first such law in Australia. It is a legitimate document because it was passed by the Parliament of Victoria and the original is held at Victoria's Registrar-General's Office.

1 Draw arrows from each bullet point in the Analysis box to the relevant example in the *Chinese Immigration Act* box.

2 Underline the sentences in the information about your birth certificate and the documents found in the National Archives that give an evaluation of the documents.

3 In the box, write what a *document* is and what *document analysis and evaluation* is.

 ISBN 9780170367141

UNIT 35
SETTING

setting = the 3 Ps (people, place, period) that make up the surroundings or environment of an event

Example: the setting of tropical cyclone Tracy

The **people** involved were the people who lived in Darwin, especially the 66 who were killed, the 645 who were injured and the 35 000 who were made homeless and had to be evacuated.

The **place** was Darwin in the Northern Territory.

The **period** was 1974 (1.00 a.m., 25 December).

Corbis/Bettmann

1 In each of the following, underline the people, the place and the period that make up the setting.

On 11 June 1964, at 2.53 a.m., the Beatles' BOAC Boeing 707 touched down in Darwin. Four hundred fans were there to greet the plane, which was on a brief stop before flying on to Sydney. Only three of the four Beatles were on board – John Lennon, Paul McCartney and George Harrison. The fourth Beatle, Ringo Starr, was still in hospital.

In 1912, Captain Scott reached the South Pole. Captain Oates was weak and slowing the other four down. Scott wrote in his diary, 'Captain Oates said, "I am just going outside and may be some time". He went into the blizzard and we have not seen him since. We knew he was walking to his death but though we tried to dissuade him, we knew it was the act of a brave man and an English gentleman'.

For 12 years, people in Singapore had not been allowed to chew gum. The ban was to keep streets, buildings, buses and trains clean. In 2004, Singapore was in free-trade talks with the USA. Chewing gum giant Wrigley put pressure on Singapore to lift its ban. A new law allowed gum to be sold, but only at chemists and buyers had to give their names and identity cards.

The fighting in Europe during the Second World War ended in May 1945. But Japan was still fighting. The USA had secretly developed the atomic bomb as a weapon. The President had to decide whether to invade Japan by sea and lose maybe a million soldiers, or to use the atom bomb to knock Japan out of the war. On 6 August 1945, a US bomber dropped an atomic bomb on the city of Hiroshima in Japan

2 In the box, write or draw what *setting* means.

ISBN 9780170367141

UNIT 36
CONTEXT

Example:
SARS (Severe Acute Respiratory Syndrome) broke out in China in 2002. It spread to other countries and hundreds of people died. Many people in Australia, and other places, could not understand how China let SARS spread around the world. But when SARS was seen in the Chinese context, it was easy to understand how it happened. The context was China's culture of silence, its health system and the size of its population. Chinese authorities knew about SARS for months before they let the world know. Millions of Chinese live in the countryside and they are very poor. They live closely with animals. There is a shortage of hospitals and doctors. The authorities handled the outbreak of SARS in a much slower and more secretive way than authorities in Australia probably would have. Australia's population of about 24 million people was much easier to keep track of than China's population of well over a billion people.

context = the time and place, and how people thought and behaved, in which an event happens

1 Today when we look back on events from the past, we ask questions. But at the time of the events, most people did not ask them. They never dreamt of asking such questions.

a Find and underline all the questions in the following boxes.

b Find the boxes without questions and label them 'context'.

c Choose a method to match each context with a question, e.g. arrows, numbers, colours. Use your method to match them up.

The First World War (1914–1918) was brutal. Men drowned in mud on battlefields. Shells blew them up. Machine guns mowed them down. Torpedoes slammed into their boats. More than 20 million people died. Yet in 1914 many people saw the war as a great adventure. HOW COULD THEY HAVE THAT ATTITUDE TO WAR?

A law banned blacks from sitting in the front part of buses. They had to pay at the front, then get into the bus by the back door. If the front part for whites was full, blacks had to give up their seats. The police arrested Rosa. Many people stopped using the buses in sympathy with her.

They had no scientific instruments. They had not explored. Their stories had expressions such as 'to the ends of the Earth', 'the four corners of the world' and 'the sun sank into the sea'.

In the Middle Ages, people gave the name 'witch' to women who did different things, such as practising herbal medicine. Many so-called witches were burned at the stake. HOW COULD PEOPLE TREAT OTHERS THIS WAY?

In 1918 the Russian Revolution was taking place. The Emperor of Russia, known as the Tsar, and his family were murdered. They were shot, bayoneted, bludgeoned and dropped into a mineshaft. Then they were dug up, mutilated further, and reburied in a pit on a deserted dirt road. For many years, there was a rumour that Anastasia, the youngest daughter of the Tsar, had escaped. HOW COULD PEOPLE BELIEVE THAT?

People used to believe that the Earth was flat. HOW COULD THEY BELIEVE THAT?

People had not seen what damage the new weapons could do. The pace of life was much slower and young men saw war as a challenge to test their bravery. They were taught to follow orders without question, never give up and the idea of '*Dulce et decorum est pro patria mori*' (It is sweet and glorious to die for your country).

People were used to burning as a punishment. They did not understand that others, who had special powers, were just people like them; they thought they must be wicked.

In 1955 a black lady called Rosa Parks sat on a bus in Montgomery in the USA. The driver asked her to give up her seat to a white person. Rosa refused. This event sparked the Civil Rights Movement in the USA. HOW COULD SUCH AN EVENT START SUCH A BIG MOVEMENT?

The country was in an uproar. The executions happened in a hurry. There were no formal records kept.

 ISBN 9780170367141

UNIT 37
PERSPECTIVE

Your perspective

This is your views and actions on issues such as drugs and banning certain breeds of dogs, or events such as space exploration and terrorist acts.

perspective = a word that comes from Latin *perspectus*, meaning looked through; what makes you see and understand events, ideas, points of view, attitudes and beliefs in the particular way that you do

Examples of things that influence your perspective:

- Country (e.g. Australia, the USA, New Zealand)
- Culture (e.g. Aboriginal, Greek, Chinese)
- Gender (e.g. male, female, transgender)
- Status (e.g. respected or hated or tolerated by society)
- Age (e.g. 12, 23, 57)
- Socioeconomic position (e.g. poor, rich, average)
- Religion (e.g. Muslim, Christian, no religion)
- Groups to which you belong (e.g. Scouts Australia, Australian Youth Orchestra, Labor Party)
- History (e.g. events that have affected you, such as war, natural disaster, climate)

1 Add labels to show why your perspective on the Vietnam War in the 1960s may have been different from that of someone else.

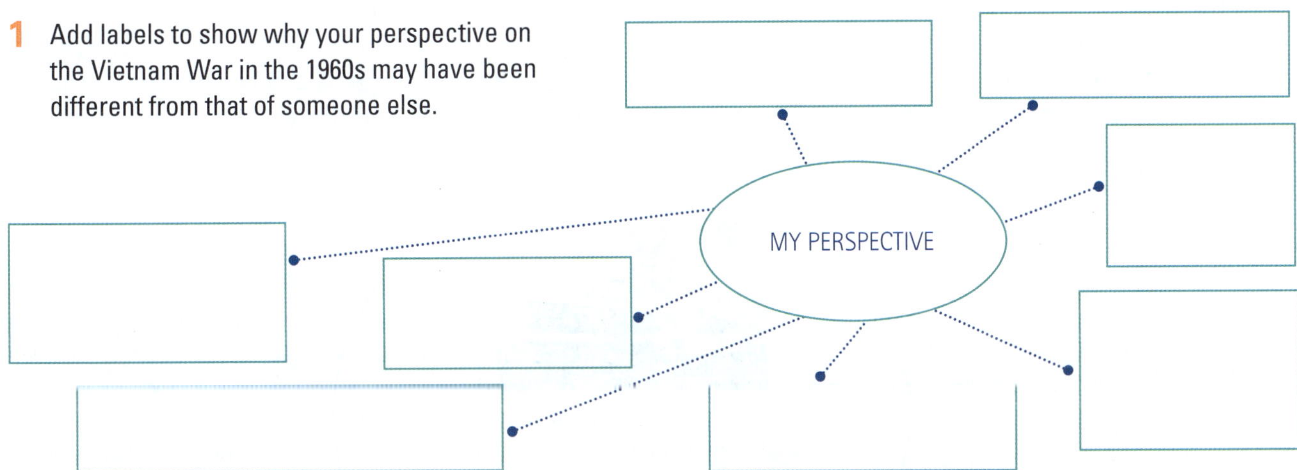

2 Suggest why the following people might have different perspectives on the same event.

Event = The opening of an uranium mine beside a National Park in Australia

a Mel is a refugee from the war in Bosnia. She is a park warden and loves the peace of the park.

____

b Stefano is an unemployed father of five children. ______________________________

c Parri is 12 years old and belongs to an anti-mining group. ______________________________

3 In the box, write or draw what *perspective* means.

ISBN 9780170367141

UNIT 38
GETTING INTO ROLE (EMPATHY)

Examples:

You imagine that instead of being a modern student, you are a teenager living in Dublin (Ireland) in 1916 and you get involved in a rebellion called 'The Easter Uprising' against British rule in Ireland.

OR

You imagine that instead of being a modern student, you are a person living in New South Wales, Australia, in 1918 during the influenza epidemic (Spanish flu), which killed millions of people around the world.

role = a person's job or function

getting into role = imagining yourself as someone else at a particular time

empathetic understanding = an understanding of the ideas and values of people in the past that led them to take particular actions or adopt particular perspectives

Things to think about when getting into role

- **The times:** If you are pretending to be someone in Australia in 1918, you need to forget about TV, PlayStations, iPhones, computers and modern antibiotics because none of those things had been invented.
- **The people:** Soldiers coming back from the First World War on transport ships were held in quarantine. The government made the wearing of masks compulsory in shops, hotels, churches, theatres and on public transport. Shops were not allowed to hold sales. Thousands of people died from the flu.
- **The effect of the event on the person:** One shopkeeper might be annoyed because of the ban on sales; another might be pleased because she had a big supply of masks. An orphaned child will be sad. A doctor will be exhausted. A scientist may be frantically looking for a cure. A church minister will be out visiting all day or holding funerals. A soldier might be desperate to see his family.

Shutterstock.com/ Everett Historical

In 1915, during the First World War, a German U-boat fired two torpedoes into a British passenger and cargo ship called the *Lusitania*. The ship sank. More than a thousand people drowned, including some Americans. At that stage, the USA was not in the war. (It joined in 1917.)

- German newspaper editor claimed ship was carrying arms and said sinking was a great success.
- Survivor pleaded for the USA to join war effort against Germany and said 'Remember the *Lusitania*.'
- Steward said 'passengers were at lunch when attack came, officials acted bravely, and sinking ship was dreadful sight'.
- Editor of a British newspaper was furious at the attack on 'innocent and defenceless people'.
- Friend of American millionaire Alfred Vanderbilt, who drowned, spoke of how Alfred gave his life jacket to a young woman even though he could not swim.
- US President sent a note of protest to German Kaiser (Emperor).
- Walther Schweiger, captain of the German U-boat that sank the ship, was delighted at the victory.

1 List some of the roles that you play in life.

2 Highlight or colour the role you would choose to play in the *Lusitania* sinking and beside it write at least five words that would show your character's opinion.

3 In the box, write what *getting into role* means.

ISBN 9780170367141

UNIT 39
MOVEMENTS

movement = people acting together in a group to bring about change

Example:

The hippie (hippy) movement of the 1960s and 1970s spread to Australia. Hippies wanted changes in society, such as getting people back to the land, living and working cooperatively, alternative energy, organic farming, and they had less interest in buying material goods. They wore flowers in their hair and gave flowers to passersby. They drove 'flower power' buses decorated with flowers and slogans such as 'Make Love Not War'. They made speeches against Australia being involved in the Vietnam War. They talked of dropping out of society and tuning in to their inner minds, with or without drugs and meditation.

Fairfax Syndication/The Sydney Morning Herald

Examples of other movements:

	Aims of the movements
Land Rights	Muslims working to get rights for Muslims in India, which was mainly Hindu ______
Federation	Aboriginal and Torres Strait Islanders in Australia working to keep their land ______
Anti-slavery	Women, and men, working to get women the right to vote ______
Anti-apartheid	In America, non-communists accused communists of being disloyal to the USA ______
Suffrage	People who wanted the colonies of Australia joined together worked to get this ______
Hitler Youth	Protesters working to stop Australia being involved in the Vietnam War ______
Sons of Liberty	German Nazis working to train young people to be loyal Nazis ______
Anti-war	Italians working to join Italian states together as one country ______
Muslim League	People who did not believe in slavery working to get rid of slavery in the world ______
Temperance	People who want world peace working to get rid of weapons of mass destruction ______
Satyagraha	Groups, mainly women, working to get alcohol banned ______
Anti-uranium	Settlers in America fighting to get rid of the British who ruled them ______
McCarthyism	World-wide groups working to get rid of separation of races in South Africa ______
Peace	People against nuclear power working to stop uranium mining in Australia ______
Young Italy	Indians using non-violence and non-cooperation to get rid of British rule ______

1 Look at the aims of the movements above. Choose the name of the associated movement and write it in the space.

2 For each aim, use one colour to circle the people in the groups wanting change and another colour to circle the change that they wanted.

3 In the box, write or draw what *movements* are.

UNIT 40
ACTION

action = something done or being done

Example:

One of Tamsin's actions in relation to Japanese planes attacking Darwin in 1942 was to take herself and her three young children to stay with her sister in Sydney. Tamsin explained why she chose to take this particular action: 'Darwin was in chaos. At least 243 people had been killed. Many more were injured. The Japanese had sunk ships, destroyed planes and wrecked most of the essential services. I had to keep my children safe. I was scared the Japanese would come back'.

Australian War Memorial (012699)

One of Ming's actions in relation to the announcement in 2015 that her town on the edge of the outback had been chosen as the place for a huge new medical research centre, was to start designing the new centre. Ming explained why she chose to take this particular action: 'As an architect, I am so excited about this area being chosen. It has a good climate, a fine water supply and great natural beauty. I thought the competition being run to find the best design for the new centre would attract architects from all over Australia. It would be such an honour to have my plan considered'.

Shutterstock.com/Kwanbenz

One of Eti's actions in relation to the 2002 terrorist bombs in the Indonesian island of Bali was to cancel his upcoming holiday to Bali. Eti explained why he chose to take this particular action: 'As an Australian, I was deeply shocked that 88 innocent Australians had been killed by terrorists. I had been to Bali before for a holiday and thought it was a wonderful place. But the terrorists have ruined it now. I don't know how long it will take before tourists, especially Australians, feel safe enough to go back to Bali'.

One of Jo's actions in relation to blacks struggling for civil rights in the USA in 1963 was to join the rally at the Lincoln Memorial in Washington, DC to hear Martin Luther King speak. Jo explained why she chose to take this particular action: 'I think the Ku Klux Klan's idea of white supremacy and white control is evil. I think the Jim Crow laws, where blacks are discriminated against just because of their colour, are evil. I think segregation where there are separate facilities for blacks and whites, is evil. I think President Kennedy's Civil Rights bill to give blacks more rights should be passed'.

Corbis/Bettmann

ISBN 9780170367141

1 Give the three words that the first sentences about Tamsin, Ming, Eti and Jo have in common that mean 'to do with'.

2 Think of an event that happened to you or you were involved in that might be of interest to a historian in future years.

a Name the event.

b Name an action that you took in relation to that event.

c Explain why you chose to take that particular action.

3 Finish the following sentences by getting into role (having empathetic understanding) and imagining you were the person living at the time.

a As an American sailor, one of my actions in relation to the Japanese attack on the American base at Pearl Harbor in 1941 was

I chose to take this particular action because

b As an Australian cricket fan in 1949, one of my actions in relation to the news that cricket legend Donald Bradman had been knighted was

I chose to take this particular action because

4 In the box, write or draw what you think an *action* is.

UNIT 41
SOCIAL FORCE

force = the power to influence

Example:
A tidal wave is a physical force. When it hits you, it has the power to influence you physically. It may turn your house into matchsticks. It may sweep you up and drop you in the top of a tree. It may leave mud over your garden. It may put you off going to any more disaster movies for years.

Corbis

social force = the name for a general idea that has an influence on the social lives of people the same way that a physical force has an influence on the physical lives of people

Example:
Imperialism is a social force. It is about one country taking over foreign lands. The country's foreign lands are called its empire. For example, Britain once practised imperialism. It ruled Australia and many other places such as New Zealand, Canada and India. These places were part of the British Empire. The British king or queen was the head of the British Empire. Britain made laws for its lands. It acquired these lands by capturing them in war, or by 'discovering' them, exploring them and claiming them, or by buying them. Today most of these places rule themselves. But you can still see a lot of British influence in their societies.

1 Choose the best names from the box below for the following descriptions of social forces and write them beside the descriptions.

Names of social forces: racism, religion, fascism, industrialisation, communism, feminism, democracy, nationalism, multiculturalism, internationalism

a social system based on the whole community sharing all work and property ____________

b demanding the right for your country to have full independence ____________

c setting up industries on a large scale ____________

d government of a country by its own people through an elected parliament ____________

e seeing the universe as having a special nature and purpose ____________

f treating people of different races differently ____________

g having several different cultures coexisting in one country ____________

h working for equal (same as male) rights and opportunities for females ____________

i nations cooperating ____________

j government controls all and cuts down on individual freedom ____________

2 In the box, write what a *social force* is.

 ISBN 9780170367141

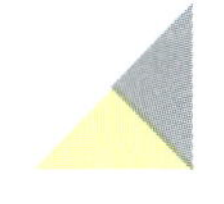

UNIT 42
HISTORICAL CONVENTIONS

conventions = common ways of doing things, saying things, writing things, seeing things

historical conventions = conventions that were around at the time in history you are talking about

Conventions change with the times. If you were living in Australia more than 100 years ago:

- you would have a very formal relationship with your teachers and never call them by their Christian names, even after you left school (possibly at the age of 12).
- if you were a male and you were walking with a female, you would make sure that you walked on the edge of the footpath closest to the road – to protect her from the mud off the street and slops thrown from upstairs windows; you would wear a hat and raise it when you greeted a female and stand up when a female entered a room.
- you would buy items with pounds, shillings and pence instead of dollars and cents.
- you would be astonished to see women being allowed to vote (Australian women had just been given the vote).
- you would use British spelling, terms and names rather than American.
- you would use and read the word 'servant' to describe live-in help.
- your newspaper would be filled with text and only the occasional photo (always black and white), map or drawing.
- for entertainment you would listen to politicians making speeches on outside platforms called *hustings*.
- on Christmas Day you would go to church and listen to the minister read out the King's or Queen's Message.

Australia changed to its present decimal currency in 1966. Until then, the currency was based on the British unit which is the pound (£) divided into 20 shillings (s.) each of 12 pence (d.).

A jingle about the change was sung to the tune of the famous Australian folk song 'Click Go The Shears':

In come the dollars, in come the cents,
To replace the pounds and the shillings
and the pence.
Be prepared folks when the coins begin
to mix
On the 14th of February 1966.

Some old documents you read will use the old currency.

one pound = £1.0.0 (one pound, no shillings and no pence) = a quid = 2 dollars =

20 shillings = 240 pennies

one shilling = 1/- = 12 pence or pennies = a 'bob' = 10 cents

one penny = about 1 cent

sixpence = 6d = 6 pence or 6 pennies = a 'zack' = 5 cents

threepence = 3d = 3 pence or pennies = a 'trey' = about 2 cents

ten shillings = 1 dollar; 5 shillings = 50 cents

1 Work out what the following would be worth in today's currency.

a £2 ____________ **b** £1 10 shillings ____________ **c** £5 ____________

d 2 shillings ____________ **e** a zack ____________ **f** 3 bob ____________

2 Give a reason why knowing about and using historical conventions of the 1920s would help you get a good mark for a piece of work about life in the 1920s.

____

____

3 In the box, write what *historical conventions* are.

ISBN 9780170367141

UNIT 43
BEING RELEVANT

relevant = to do with a subject; the opposite of relevant is irrelevant

Example:

A student wrote about the ship called the *Titanic* and its passengers:

The *Titanic* was the largest and most luxurious passenger liner of its day. Its owners claimed it was the safest ship afloat. In 1912 it set sail from England, bound for New York. Leonardo DiCaprio, who starred in a movie about the *Titanic*, is a big Hollywood star. In the Atlantic Ocean the *Titanic* hit an iceberg. The 'unsinkable' liner sank quickly. There were not enough lifeboats for everyone. More than 1500 people died.

All the sentences, except the one underlined, are about the ship called *Titanic*. The underlined sentence about Leonardo DiCaprio is not relevant. Instead, it is irrelevant.

1 Underline the sentence in each of the following that is not relevant.

Australian Edward 'Ned' Trickett won the World Sculling Championship in 1876. The event was held on London's River Thames. In the olden days, Danish pirates used to go up and down the River Thames, stealing from other ships. Trickett became Australia's first big sporting star. The news of his victory took three weeks to reach Sydney. When he arrived home in Sydney, 25 000 people waited to greet him.

State Library of Victoria

Australia's largest search. In 1937, a Stinson Model A Airliner left Brisbane for Sydney. It had two crew and five passengers. It failed to arrive in Sydney. Some people said Sydney should have been the national capital rather than Canberra. This caused the largest air search in Australia's peace-time history. A week later, the official search was called off. Bernard O'Reilly was a young bushman. He decided to search. He found the wreck of the plane. Two men were still alive – 10 days after the plane had crashed.

Artefacts go home to Aborigines. In 2004, the Museum of South Australia returned some fire sticks to the Warumungu people of Tennant Creek. The Museum has six floors of exhibits and many favourite places such as the ancient Egypt room. The fire sticks were described as simple, but beautiful and delicate, instruments. They had been used by a man called Dick Cubadgee Jappangarti. Cubadgee was explorer Dick Lindsay's guide and interpreter in the 1880s. The elders who accepted the fire sticks handled them gently and with respect and admiration. They spoke in their own language.

Young Australian soldiers died on the Kokoda Trail. The Kokoda Trail was in Papua. It was a muddy and rough foot track over the Owen Stanley Range. In 1942, Japanese troops landed on Papua. The Japanese kamikaze pilots in the war deliberately crashed their planes with bombs in them. The Japanese troops decided to march over the Kokoda Trail to capture Port Moresby. Australian soldiers fought them on the trail. The Australians pushed the Japanese back over the Owen Stanley Range. About 625 Australian soldiers were killed on the trail. More than 1600 were wounded.

2 In the box, write what *being relevant* means.

ISBN 9780170367141

UNIT 44
BIAS

bias = prejudice; a strong feeling towards or against

Examples:

Julius Caesar was biased towards Cleopatra because he admired beauty and she was very beautiful.

Mark Antony's wife was biased against Cleopatra because Mark Antony ran off with Cleopatra.

Historians try to be unbiased (or objective) when they write secondary resources about the past. They try not to let their personal feelings affect what they write, so they keep to the truth about what happened.

Many primary sources are biased. They are created by people; and people have biases. The sources tell us only what the creator thought happened. Or they tell us only what the creator wants us to think happened.

1 Read about the introduction in 1935 of the cane toad, a native of the Americas, into Queensland. Put a cross beside the sentences that seem to be biased.

☐ **a** It was supposed to control the beetle that attacks sugar cane but it became a pest and is still spreading.

☐ **b** Its glands give out a fluid called bufotoxin that is dangerous to many animals, including humans.

☐ **c** It should be let loose on the people who brought it in to Australia.

☐ **d** It has been known to try to eat ping pong balls, which shows how stupid it is.

2 Your school report is a resource. A historian of the future might use it to write about you. Give the following details about one of your recent reports.

a the source of the resource ______

b the reason the resource was created ______

c whether the resource was created through a spur-of-the-moment act, or a thoughtful, planned process

______

d whether the resource was written by people who did not know you, or by people who had opinions that might have influenced what they wrote ______

e whether the resource was created to be private or public ______

f whether the resource was written by people with first-hand experience of the subject (you) or by people who relied on what others said ______

g whether the information was recorded during the term, or much later ______

3 In the box, write what you think *bias* is.

UNIT 45
AMBIGUITY

ambiguity = having two or more possible meanings

Examples:

The French teacher took an instant liking to his bright pupil Archimedes. (The sentence is ambiguous because you do not know if it was a teacher who taught French as a subject, or a teacher who came from France.)

Queen Mary had her bottom scraped. (The sentence is ambiguous because Queen Mary was the name of a person and also the name of a ship.)

Here are some historically famous ambiguous headlines

Man eating piranha mistakenly sold as pet fish

Officials put foot down on dog waste

Genetic engineering splits scientists

Arson suspect is held in fire

Grandmother of eight makes hole in one

Local high school dropouts cut in half

Squad helps dog bite victim

Lawmen from Mexico barbeque guests

1 Making as few changes as possible, rewrite the following so that they are no longer ambiguous.

- **a** The driver glanced at Hitler and headed over the bank.
- **b** In an effort to kill a bee Ben Hur drove his chariot into a tree.
- **c** Friar Tuck had been riding for three months when he fell asleep and crashed his horse.
- **d** After the President watched the chimp perform, he was taken to Queen Street and fed two buckets full of bananas.
- **e** Sue Smith visited the school and lectured on 'Nasty Pests'. A lot were present.
- **f** The Governor-General smashed the champagne against the prow at the launching and the crowd cheered as she slid down the runway into the tide.
- **g** Protestors released rats in Parliament, and these were arrested when they left.
- **h** Violence took centre stage at the Supreme Court.

2 In the box, write why you should avoid being *ambiguous*.

 ISBN 9780170367141

UNIT 46
FACT AND OPINION

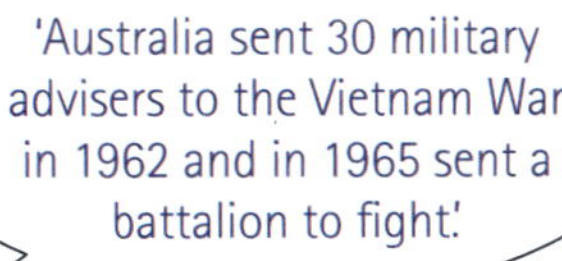

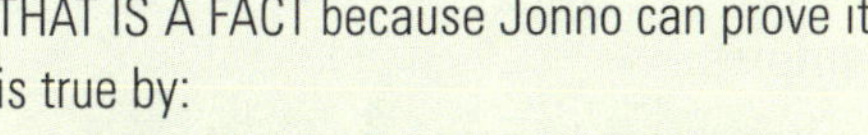

THAT IS A FACT because Jonno can prove it is true by:
- showing it is written in official books
- talking to people who were part of the military advisers and battalion
- showing it is pictured in newsreels of the time.

THAT IS AN OPINION because Lara cannot prove it is true as:
- many people do not agree with her
- she is saying what she thinks should not have happened, rather than what did happen.

1 Cross out some words that Lara said so you change her opinion into a fact.

2 Read the comments below about a famous Australian explorer named Douglas Mawson. Colour the facts one colour and the opinions another colour.

He was born in 1882 and died in 1958.

He was two when his family moved to Australia from England.

At school, he was a bright student.

He was interested in nature and how the Earth was formed.

He made trips of exploration to Antarctica.

He thought it was important for Australians to be involved in finding out about Antarctica.

It was hard to raise money for the trips to Antarctica.

Once he had to eat his huskies to survive.

He should have been made Sir Douglas before 1914.

It is fitting that his face appears on the $100 note.

He was knighted in 1914 for his contribution to the scientific understanding of Antarctica.

3 In the box, write the difference between *fact and opinion*.

UNIT 47
ANACHRONISM

anachronism = putting something or someone in the wrong time accidentally; usually happens when the wrong time is too early for the thing or person to have been around in

Examples:

A writer refers to a peasant in the fourteenth century using a mobile phone to call for help when wolves attack. That is an anachronism because mobiles were not invented until the late twentieth century.

A director makes a movie about Joan of Arc, who was burned at the stake in 1431. The director accidentally includes a tractor in a scene. That is an anachronism because tractors were not invented until the late nineteenth century.

An artist paints a village feast in the year 1600 and shows children eating ice-cream in cones. That is an anchronism because cones were not invented until the late nineteenth century.

1 Put a cross through the anachronism in the following sets of pictures (there is one in each).

a Weapons of the First World War 1914–1918

      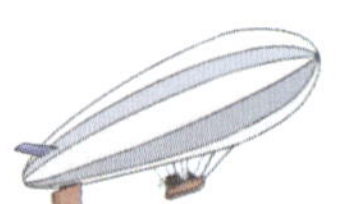

b The French Revolution of 1789

c Medieval England

d Highwayman Dick Turpin of the eighteenth century

2 In the box, write what an *anachronism* is.

ISBN 9780170367141

UNIT 48
CHRONOLOGY

chron/chrono = time

logy = the study of

chronology = a record of events in the order in which they happened; important so the reader or viewer knows the order in which events happened

Alamy/GL Archive

Example: The capture of Ned Kelly, Aussie outlaw, in 1880

Ned decided to ambush the train that was carrying the police who were after him. He and his gang forced railwaymen to tear up the track several metres from the station at Glenrowan. The gang rounded up people from the town as hostages and held them at the hotel. The local school teacher escaped from the hotel and flagged the train down to warn the policemen. Early in the morning the police began to battle with the gang in the hotel. Ned put on a metal helmet and armour and slipped out the back of the hotel. At dawn, Ned loomed up behind the police lines. The police fired but the bullets bounced off Ned's armour. Finally, a bullet hit Ned's leg. Ned fell and the police captured him.

1 The following are milestones in the life of Joan of Arc. She was famous for being a brilliant and brave leader and heroine, and for coming to the rescue of France during a war against England, known as the 100 Year War. Sort the milestones into chronological order.

a As Joan had never seen the Dauphin, he stood among his nobles to test her.

b After Orleans, Joan led France to many victories.

c In 1429 she returned and persuaded the Commandant to give her permission to go to the Dauphin.

d The English put Joan on trial and she was called a witch, and accused of wearing men's clothing and disobeying her parents and the teachings of the church.

e When she was 16, Joan went to the Commandant of a town near her village and asked him to send her to the Dauphin. He sent her home.

f She was born in 1412 in France.

g Joan picked the Dauphin out immediately among the nobles and she was given command of an army to go and help Orleans, which the English were attacking. Joan put on armour, inspired the troops to follow her and saved Orleans.

h In 1430, French soldiers fighting on the side of the English captured Joan and sold her to the English.

i Joan was burned at the stake in 1431.

j When Joan was 12 years old, she began to hear voices and see visions of saints who told her she must go to the French court and help the Dauphin (heir to the throne).

2 In the box, write or draw what *chronology* is.

ISBN 9780170367141

UNIT 49
OBITUARY

obituary = a notice of the death of a person (e.g. printed in a newspaper); often includes a story about the person's life

You might be asked to write an obituary of a person, real or made-up.

Tips on writing an obituary

Getty Images/AFP/Torsten Blackwood

say who the person was

give date of birth

give date of death

say if the person is survived by any close family

say where the person lived and note any significant achievements

use formal language and be respectful

write the truth in a way that does not give offence

Kerry Packer 17 December 1937 – 26 December 2005

Kerry Francis Bullmore Packer, younger son of Sydney media mogul Sir Frank Packer, has died. He is survived by his wife, Roslyn Redman Weedon, his son James and his daughter Gretel.

The Packer name in Sydney began at the turn of the nineteenth century when Kerry Packer's grandfather, Tasmanian-born Robert Clyde Packer, arrived in Sydney at 21. Kerry became chairman of a media empire in 1974, when he was 37.

Kerry Packer was Australia's wealthiest person with a fortune estimated at A$7 billion. He was an important media and property owner, and was also clever at politics. He began a sporting revolution in 1977 when he introduced World Series Cricket.

He was criticised for bullying and swearing. Admirers praised his charm and generosity.

Poliomyelitis struck him when he was eight years old. He spent nine months in an iron lung. He also suffered from dyslexia. His father called him 'boofhead'. He went to Australia's famous private school – Geelong Grammar. It took him six years to do a four-year course. He was the school heavyweight boxing champion. He later said, 'I agree completely with my son James when he says "Internet is like electricity – the latter lights up everything, while the former lights up knowledge".'

Kerry Packer made headlines with his gambling. Australian casinos could not handle his big wagers so he did his gambling abroad. It was reported he won $24 million playing blackjack in Las Vegas in June 1995. He reportedly lost $7 million in 1987 at a Sydney race meeting.

Kerry Packer was 1.9 m and 127 kg. In 1986, he was rushed to hospital for the removal of his gall bladder and a kidney. In 1990, he had a heart attack playing polo and had to have a quintuple heart bypass. In 2000 he had a kidney transplant. His helicopter pilot and friend Nicholas Ross donated the kidney.

quote something funny or wise or interesting that the person said

the best way to describe the person and the times is by telling stories about the person

write how people at the time would have written, e.g. in 2005 the term 'media' was in use but if Packer had died 100 years ago 'media' was not in use

use the measurements that people at the time would have used, e.g. if Packer had died 100 years ago his measurements would be 6 ft 3 in and 20 stone

1 Draw arrows from each tip on writing an obituary to the place in Packer's obituary that is an example of the tip.

2 In the box, write or draw what an *obituary* is.

ISBN 9780170367141

UNIT 50
MEASURING TIME

Time words include:

aeon very long period of time
age a period of time in history, e.g. the Ice Age
anniversary yearly return of the date of an event, e.g. your birthday
antiquity any ancient time
AD *Anno Domini* (In the year of Our Lord); AD dates go forwards from year 0
ancient long ago, especially before the fall of Western Roman Empire about AD 476
BC Before Christ; BC dates go backwards from year 0
BCE Before the Common Era (alternative for BC)
c symbol meaning *circa* or 'about', e.g. 'c 1200 AD' stands for 'at about 1200 AD'
CE Common Era (alternative for AD)
century 100 years
contemporary of present time
Dark Ages about 476 AD to 1000 AD
date the year (can also include month and day) when an event took place
decade 10 years
epoch period of time seen as an important beginning
era period of time marked by distinctive events or features, e.g. the hippie era
Medieval Middle Ages about 800 AD to 1400 AD
modern history since the Renaissance
period a portion of time
pre-history time before recorded history
Renaissance rebirth of learning in Europe in fourteenth, fifteenth and sixteenth centuries
score 20 years

Some names of anniversaries

1st = annual	6th = hexennial	50th = quinquagenary or jubilee
2nd = biennial	7th = septennial	100th = centennial
3rd = triennial	8th = octennial	150th = sesquicentennial
4th = quadrennial	9th = novennial	500th = quincentennial
5th = quinquennial	10th = decennial	1000th = millennial

1 Sort the following into four related groups and then arrange them in the boxes in order of earliest to latest.

millenial, century, pre-history, the Dark Ages, octennial, BCE, modern history, score, biennial, decade, decennial, Renaissance, sesquicentennial, CE, ancient history, the Middle Ages

a | | |

b | | | | | | |

c | | | |

d | | | | | |

2 Work out what the following might stand for.

a bicentennial ____________
b septendecennial ____________
c septcentennial ____________
d quindecimillenial ____________

ISBN 9780170367141

UNIT 51
TIMELINE

timeline = events set out in a line in the order in which they happened

A timeline is often written in the present tense, e.g. '2018 I win Lotto'. Below are examples of three different timelines.

Example: Evel Knievel

Evel Knievel was a motorcycle daredevil. His stunts included riding through fire walls, jumping over live rattlesnakes and mountain lions, holding on to a parachute while being towed at fast speeds behind dragster race cars, and risking his life in a rocket-powered 'Skycycle' trying to clear a canyon. Here is part of a timeline for him.

Getty Images/Central Press

1938 born Robert Knievel in Montana

1965 forms Evel Knievel's Motorcycle Daredevils

1966 begins touring alone

1968 crashes while jumping fountains at Caesar's Palace in Las Vegas

1970 clears 13 cars in a jump

1971 jumps 19 cars

1973 jumps 50 cars

1975 clears 13 double-decker buses in London

1976 injured while jumping a tank full of live sharks in Chicago

The Domino Theory stated that communism would knock over governments one after another:

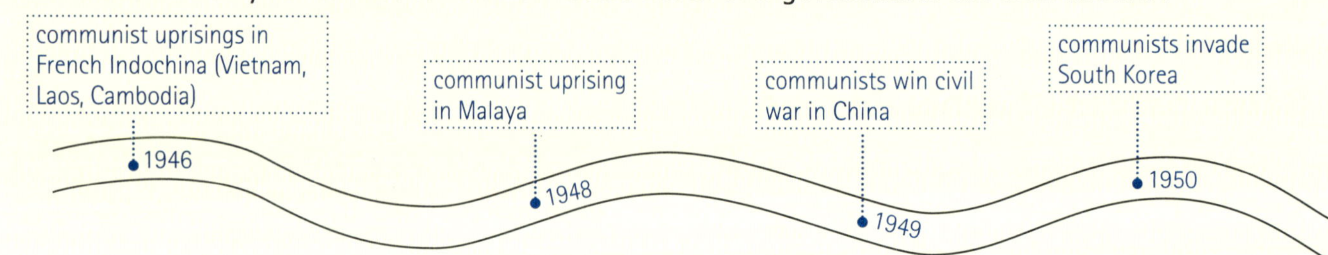

Modern Summer Olympic Games

1896	1924	1936	1948	1964	1972	1988	2000	2004	2008
Athens Greece	Paris France	Berlin Germany	London UK	Tokyo Japan	Munich Germany	Seoul South Korea	Sydney Australia	Athens Greece	Beijing China

1 On the following timeline, write six important events of your life (e.g. your birth).

2 Write down the dates that would be added to the timeline of Summer Olympic Games above if it was a complete list of all the Olympics held to 2016. (The 1940 and 1944 Olympics were cancelled because of the Second World War.)

3 In the box, write or draw what a *timeline* is.

ISBN 9780170367141

UNIT 52
KEY

key = the most important

key time

key event

key word

key sentence

key moment

key idea

key people

On Boxing Day 2004, an earthquake of magnitude 9.0, the world's biggest quake in 40 years, took place about 160 kilometres off the west coast of Indonesia. It was caused when the Indian plate – one of the tectonic plates that make up the Earth's surface – was forced under the Burma plate. The earthquake set off a tsunami that hit 12 countries in Asia, such as Thailand where the famous Phuket Island was filled with thousands of overseas tourists. Amateur videos captured the 10-metre wall of water smashing onto land. This extreme natural event brought months of disaster. More than 150 000 people were killed. Others were left homeless, starving, injured, sick and sad. People said it was the worst time since the Second World War. Governments and individuals around the world sent money for victim relief. Some tourists stayed on to help locals.

Newspix/AFP

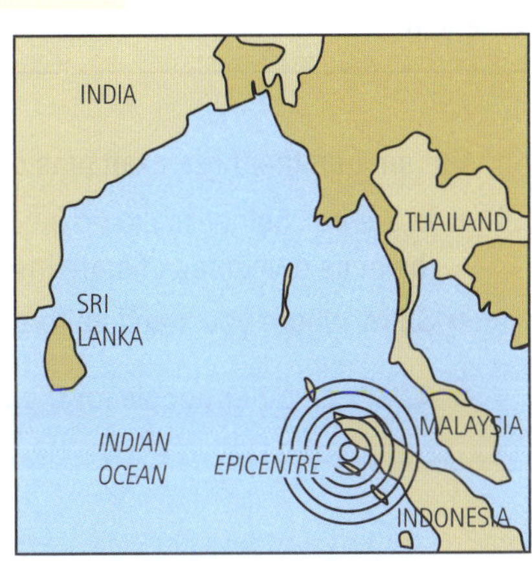

1 Give two key ways in which Australians could have been involved in the disaster.

---

2 Underline the key sentence that gives the key idea in the following story.

A 10-year-old British schoolgirl saved the lives of hundreds of people in southern Asia by warning them that a wall of water was about to strike. She had learnt about tsunamis from her teacher at school. She was on the beach when the water went bubbly and the tide suddenly went out. She raised the alert. The beach and hotel were evacuated before the tsunami hit.

3 In the box, write or draw what *key* means.

ISBN 9780170367141

UNIT 53
CONTINUUM

One way to show how people have different opinions on historical issues is by using a continuum.

continuum
- [Latin] something without breaks
- said as kon-tin-new-um
- a continuous range between two extremes (end points)

Examples:

Timelines – showing historical events, e.g. when the historic event of your birth took place.

1985 1990 1995 2000 2005 2010

Options – where people stand on issues, e.g. opinions on whether or not movies teach us about history.

a lot nothing

OR

always sometimes never

Rating – e.g. what you thought of the last historical movie you saw

excellent average bad

1 Put an X on the three examples of continuums above to show your position on them.

2 a In the box below, make up a continuum to show opinions on whether or not Australia should become a republic (have its own head of state instead of the Queen).

b Show where you stand on this issue.

c Ask three other people for their opinions, and show them on your continuum.

3 In the box, write or draw what a *continuum* is.

ISBN 9780170367141

UNIT 54
STORYBOARD

storyboard = a graphic (drawing) of events in the order they happened

Example:

The causes of the Second World War (1939–1945) are written in prose (writing) like this:

In 1935, Hitler began to build up Germany's army, even though a treaty signed by Germany at the end of the First World War had forbidden it. In 1936, Hitler began to build a large fleet and an air force, even though these were also forbidden by the treaty. Germany signed a treaty with Italy and Japan in 1936. Civil war (war inside a country, often between government forces and rebel forces) broke out in Spain in 1936. Germany and Italy tried out their new weapons and planes by helping the Spanish rebels. In 1938, Germany took over Austria. In 1939, Germany seized Czechoslovakia and signed a treaty with Russia. On 1 September 1939, Hitler's troops marched into Poland to take it over. Britain and France gave Hitler 24 hours to get out of Poland. When Hitler refused, Britain and France declared war on Germany.

The storyboard below contains the causes of the Second World War. (The artist has drawn them correctly but put them in the wrong order.)

1 Number the pictures of the storyboard 1 to 8 to show the order in which they should appear.

2 Make up a storyboard to show the following points about part of the history of Alice Springs in Central Australia.

Alice Springs (Mparntwe), home to the Arrernte Aboriginal people; 1862 explorer John Stuart on expedition north (town that grew where Alice Springs is, named Stuart); 1872 telegraph line from Adelaide to Darwin, office at Stuart called Alice Springs; 1883 miners came for garnet (red-coloured gemstones); 1887 miners came for gold; Afghan camel trains from Oodnadatta railhead; 1929 Adelaide–Stuart railway line; 1933 Stuart renamed Alice Springs.

3 In the box, write or draw what a *storyboard* is.

ISBN 9780170367141

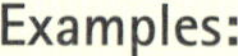

UNIT 55

HISTORICAL INVESTIGATION

Examples:

a historical investigation into the sport of surfing

a historical investigation into the assassination of US President Kennedy

a historical investigation into the Bermuda Triangle

a historical investigation into what caused the First World War

a historical investigation into an early settler from your local community

historical investigation = a careful examination of a topic

Steps to follow for a historical investigation:

1 State what your investigation is going to be about. This is called *defining areas of enquiry*. (see Unit 57)

2 Make up questions to help you collect information. This is called *making up focusing questions*. (see Unit 58)

3 Make a plan for how you will do your investigation. This is called *making a plan for the enquiry*. (see Unit 59)

4 Find information from sources and decide which bits you will use. This is called *gathering and selecting historical information*. (see Unit 60)

5 Keep a record of everything you do for your investigation and everything you find. This is called *keeping a log*. (see this Unit)

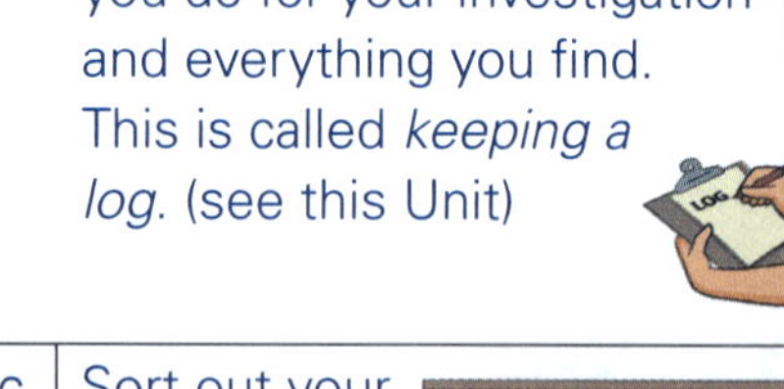

6 Sort out your information and put it in order of how useful it is as evidence to support your conclusions. This is called *organising and ranking historical information*. (see Units 61 and 62)

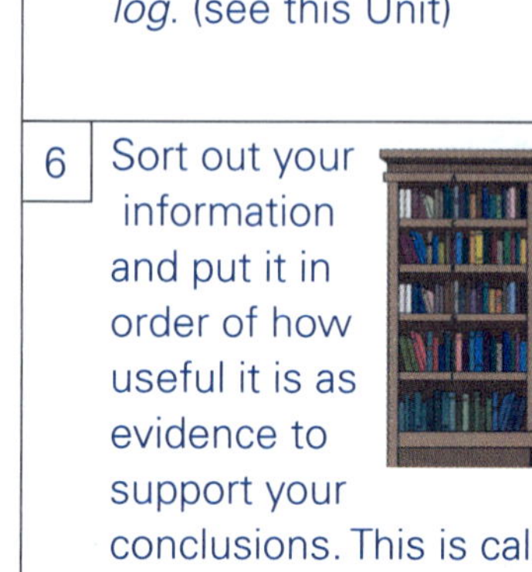

7 Put your information into the format and style you have been asked to, ready to give to your teacher for marking. This is called *using appropriate format and style*. (see Unit 33)

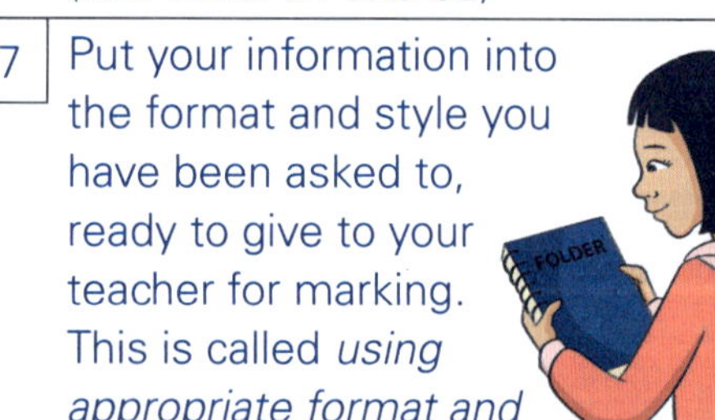

8 Say how well your enquiry went. This is called *evaluating the enquiry*. (see Unit 63)

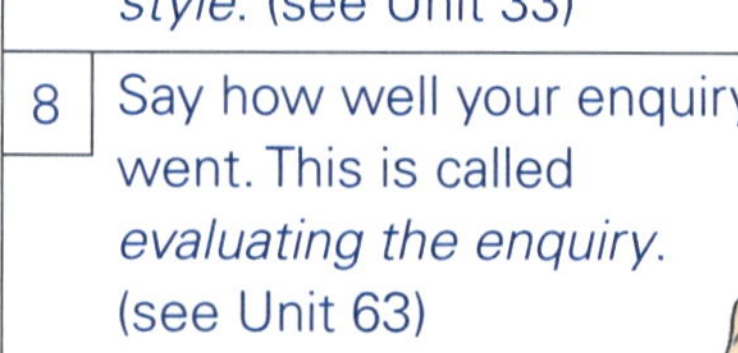

ISBN 9780170367141

A log is short for logbook. It is a record of how things are going. Sailors keep a log of their sea voyages. History students keep a log of their historical voyages. They do this so they have a record of every piece of evidence. This helps them become focused and organised.

Notes to put in your log:

- how the evidence helps a focusing question and to which focusing question it relates
- name of source
- type of source
- where you found it
- who produced the source
- why was the source produced
- historical evidence selected
- other comments.

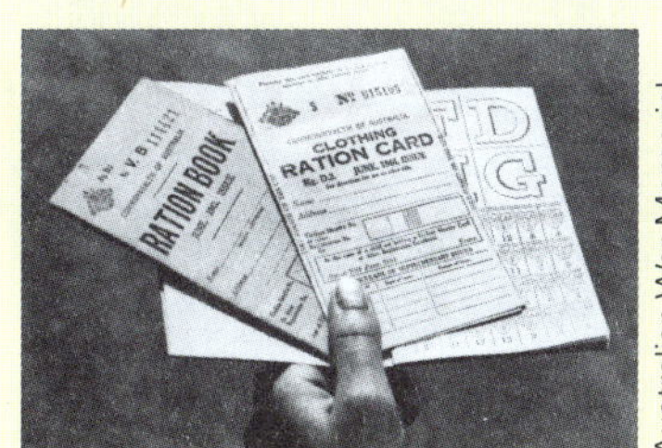

Australian War Memorial (042770)

A log entry:

Ration book from the Second World War:

- shows the effects of the war on people in Australia (I would have been starving!!!!!)
- really useful to answer my focusing question 2
- primary resource – very old paper and musty smell to prove it!
- got it from Gramps
- Gramps wants it back after I've photocopied it. He said he's got a good collection of old stuff in the trunk where he found these for me. Must ask him to explain exactly how these ration books worked, and if he has anything else in his trunk to help my investigation.

1 Historians are like detectives. In the bag, write skills this historian will use during a historical investigation.

2 Imagine you are doing a historical investigation into History Skills. Give some details of this book you could put into your log.

3 In the box, write or draw what a *historical investigation* is.

ISBN 9780170367141

UNIT 56
TAKING NOTES

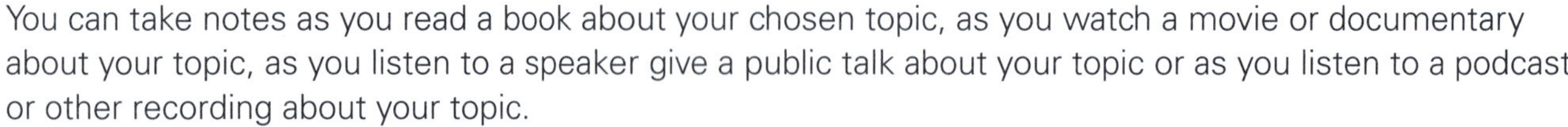

You can take notes as you read a book about your chosen topic, as you watch a movie or documentary about your topic, as you listen to a speaker give a public talk about your topic or as you listen to a podcast or other recording about your topic.

Reasons for taking notes:

- to have a record of what you heard and/or saw
- to summarise (make smaller) information
- to communicate points, ideas and information to yourself at a later time
- to communicate this information in a simple, clear and easily understood way
- to have notes to jog your memory and as a quick reference.

How to take notes:

- jot down key points only
- use your own words if they are quicker to write
- use abbreviations
- use your own shorthand – notes have to make sense only to you.

Example:

Australia's vast distances meant many people living in the outback had no medical service to help with emergencies such as accidents. A clergyman named John Flynn set up the Aerial Medical Service. Its first flight was from Cloncurry to Mt Isa in 1928 to pick up an injured youth. In 1942, the service was renamed the Flying Doctor Service. In 1955, the Queen approved 'Royal' being added to its name. So it became the Royal Flying Doctor Service.

1928 Aerial Med.
Service started
(John Flynn);
Cloncurry – Mt Isa
1942 Renamed Flying
Doctor Service
1955 Renamed Royal
Flying Doctor Service

1 Underline the main points in the following and write your notes in the box.

In 1948 communists in Malaya tried to take over the country. At this time Britain ruled Malaya. The communists had camps in the jungle. They ambushed road traffic and derailed trains. They made hit-and-run raids. They killed owners of rubber plantations, burned factories and cut rubber trees. British hunter-killer platoons fought the communists in the jungle. The British also used cunning. An example was when anybody bought a can of food, it was then punctured so the food could not be stored and given to communists.

2 Write down what the following probably stands for in notes taken from the extract in question 1.

a Brit ______ **b** e.g. ______ **c** coms ______

3 Summarise the first sentence in question 1 in five words or less.

______

4 In the box, write how to *take notes.*

ISBN 9780170367141

UNIT 57
DEFINING YOUR AREA OF ENQUIRY

Historical investigation

Example: If you are asked to do a historical investigation of Australia's First Fleet, the areas of enquiry you define must be to do with the how, why, when, what, where of the First Fleet only and not events that happened before or after.

defining = sorting out boundaries

areas = set measurements or ranges

enquiry = research to find information on a particular topic

Defining areas of enquiry sorts out boundaries for your investigation. For example, if you were told the historical investigation was about a nineteenth-century person from your local community, areas of enquiry you could define are:

▲ the reasons the person was living in your local community 	▲ milestones in the person's life 
▲ what made the person special 	▲ how people regarded the person at the time 
▲ how the person is regarded today 	▲ how the person changed or helped the local community 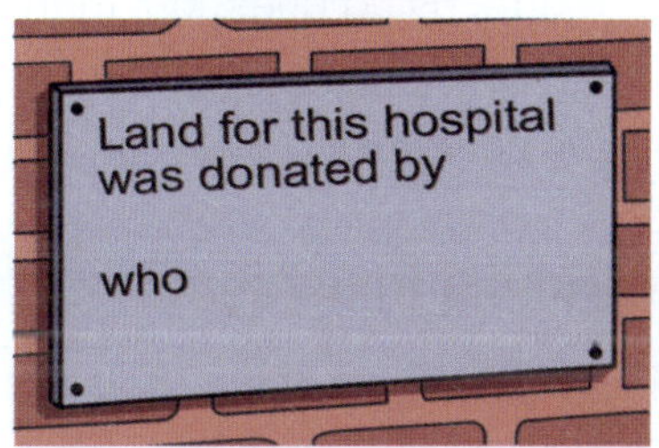

1 Your historical investigation is on the 1851 discovery of gold in Victoria. Put a tick beside the best four areas of enquiry. These will be the ones that are clearly about the 1851 discovery of gold in Victoria.

a How did the 1851 Victorian gold rush start?

b Why did Victoria become a separate colony from New South Wales in 1851?

c How did Victoria get its name?

d From where did the gold diggers come?

e What effect on the colony did the gold rush have?

f Why were the 1890s hard years for Victoria?

g How important to the colony was the 1851 gold rush?

2 In the box, write what *defining areas of enquiry* means.

ISBN 9780170367141

UNIT 58
FOCUSING QUESTIONS

Historical investigation

focusing questions = questions you make up to help you choose evidence for your historical investigation

The questions you set must be open, e.g. the words *what*, *why* and *how* are used to start the question. They let you gather a lot of information because there is no one short correct answer.

Example:
How did the sheep squatters in the Australian colony of Victoria help make Victoria rich? (There are several reasons, which need explanations.)

Avoid making up closed questions, e.g. the word *when* is used to start the question. They will let you gather only small amounts of information because there is only one short correct answer.

Example:
When did Albert Jacka become the first Australian to win the Victoria Cross? (The only correct answer is '1917'.)

Between three and six focusing questions is probably enough for most historical investigations. Too few will mean too little information. Too many will mean too much or confusing information.

- If a piece of information you collect does not help you answer the focusing question, then it is not evidence.
- If a piece of information you collect does help you answer the focusing question, then it is evidence.
- On every piece of evidence you gather, you should show which focusing question the evidence is for.

Historical investigation 1

The social effects of the 1930s Great Depression
Focusing questions could be:
How did the Great Depression affect students?
How did the Great Depression affect their parents?
How did the Great Depression affect family life?
How did the Great Depression affect communities?

Historical investigation 2

The importance of Torres Strait Islander Eddie Mabo to Australia
Focusing questions could be:
How did he become famous?
How did people regard him while he was alive?
How do people regard him today?

1 Put either 'focusing' or 'focus' in the following gaps to finish the sentences.

a Focusing questions help you to ________________ on what is important.

b You should always see if information answers your ________________ question.

2 Cross out the least useful focusing question.

a How did Australian aviator Charles Kingsford Smith die?

b When did Charles Kingsford Smith disappear?

c How did people react to the disappearance of his plane *Lady Southern Cross*?

3 In the box, write what *focusing questions* are.

 ISBN 9780170367141

UNIT 59
PLAN FOR THE ENQUIRY

Historical investigation

A plan for the enquiry shows how you are going to carry out your investigation. It might show:

▲ your focusing questions	▲ the date it has to be given to your teacher for marking
▲ all the tasks you need to do I'll brainstorm all my tasks first and put them in order later.	▲ a timeline of milestones you want to reach
▲ how much time you might need for each task I could spend an hour seeing how many of Grandma's mates would be up for interviews	▲ the times you will be free to work at the tasks I have hockey practice on Monday from 4 to 5 ...
▲ places where you think you may find information and their opening hours There's the museum, the town library, the school library, the RSA ...	▲ what type of information you expect to find The local museum has some great artefacts that I could photograph.
▲ people who could be useful to interview and what you might find out from them Aunty will be able to tell me what it was like before the wharf was built.	▲ how you will make sure you do not lose any evidence you gather I need a special folder.

1 Circle the best alternatives to finish the sentences.

a Plan means to look ahead / to look back.

b Plans of enquiry should be the same for all students / suited to the individual student.

2 You are to do a historical investigation into a person you admire, e.g. a musician or a world leader. List five things you might write down in your plan of enquiry.

a ______________________

b ______________________

c ______________________

d ______________________

e ______________________

ISBN 9780170367141

UNIT 60

GATHERING AND SELECTING HISTORICAL INFORMATION

Historical investigation

gathering = collecting

selecting = choosing the items that help you answer your focusing questions

Examples:

Maia collected her grandparents' marriage certificate and four photos of their wedding. Maia chose the certificate and two photos to use as evidence. She wrote on them the focusing question number that these were evidence for and made a note in her log.

Joss collected photocopies of three tables of statistics from the archives in the town library. Joss chose to keep one table as evidence. She wrote on them the focusing question number this evidence was for and made a note in her log.

Collecting

Choosing

Phil collected information from the Internet by taking notes from five different websites. Phil chose to keep all his notes. He wrote on them the focusing question number the evidence was for and made a note in his log.

Bev collected a modern atlas and an old atlas. Bev chose to take photocopies of two maps from each atlas. She wrote on them the number of the focusing questions the evidence was for and made a note in her log.

Manu collected a bunch of letters his great-grandfather had written. Manu chose to use three as evidence. He photocopied them and wrote on them the number of the focusing questions the evidence was for and made a note in his log.

Pi collected two photos of artefacts. Pi chose to keep one photo. He wrote on it the focusing question number the evidence was for and made a note in his log.

Rua recorded his interview with a new arrival in Australia. Rua chose to make a written copy (transcript) of the recording. He wrote on it the number of the focusing questions the evidence was for and made a note in his log.

Kris collected four books from the school library. She chose to take notes from three of them. On the notes, she wrote the number of the focusing questions the evidence was for and made a note in her log.

1 Name the four activities all students had in common.

2 Make up the note that Manu might have made in his log.

3 Make up the note that Joss might have made in her log.

4 In the box, write what *gathering and selecting historical information* means.

 ISBN 9780170367141

UNIT 61
ORGANISING HISTORICAL INFORMATION

Historical investigation

Some different ways to organise information:

Ave organised her folder using her focusing questions as headings. For example, when she gathered a piece of information that helped with her 4th focusing question, she filed that information under Focus Question 4. She then gathered information that helped with her 1st and 2nd focusing questions so she filed that information under Focus Question 1 and made a note in the margin that it could also be useful for Focus Question 2.

organise = putting together, arranging into a system or pattern

organise historical information = keep all your information in a folder; put everything you gather and select into this folder; mark the folder clearly with bright colours so it is easy to see and find

Zac organised his folder in the order in which he gathered his information. On Day 1, he gathered information from the web and he put this at the beginning of his folder. On Day 2, he gathered information from an interview, and he put this in his folder next. On Day 3, he continued to gather information and put it in the folder after Day 2's.

Dai organised her folder in the order in which different history events happened. She put her information about Australia's 1920 *Nationality Act* first. Next, she put information about the 1948 *Nationality and Citizenship Act*. Then she put her information about the 1962 *Commonwealth Electoral Act* which gave Aboriginals and Torres Strait Islanders the vote.

Harry organised his folder under headings relating to the type of sources he gathered. All the web information went under the heading of 'Internet'. All the information from interviews went under the heading of 'Interviews'. All the information from photographs went under the heading of 'Visuals', and so on.

Sel organised her folder under the headings of 'Most useful', 'Maybe useful', 'Least useful'. Notes from several books went into the 'Most useful' because they were the best at answering her focusing questions. A table of statistics went into the 'Maybe useful' because she was not sure if she would use them to answer her focusing questions. Some cartoons went into the 'Least useful' because she decided they did not help to answer the focusing questions.

1 **a** Suggest one other way you could organise your information.

____

b Decide which option you would choose, and give a reason.

____

2 Dai's folder of information was organised. Zac's folder of information was not.

a Suggest one thing that Dai had done that Zac had not done.

____

b Give one reason why Dai will seem to have better skills than Zac if they both apply for the same job.

____

3 In the box, write what *organising historical information* means.

ISBN 9780170367141

UNIT 62
RANKING HISTORICAL INFORMATION

Historical investigation

ranking = putting items or events in order of importance, e.g. Matt ranked the Harry Potter movies and found his favourite was still *Harry Potter and the Half-Blood Prince*

Example:

Rank	Where information came from and why you ranked it in this place
1	*Charles Sturt – Explorer of Australia* by W. Fry. This book uses clear language to give every possible detail about Sturt's three great expeditions: to trace the Macquarie River in 1828, to explore Murrumbidgee River in 1829 and to explore the desert country in 1844. The author is a distant relation of Sturt and writes as if he actually knew him. Despite this, he tries, and generally succeeds, to present an unbiased view. It answered all my focusing questions in the first half of the book yet I continued to read it because the author was so passionate about his evidence. No other source provided me with such quality evidence.
2	*Charles Sturt 1795–1869* by I. Duckworth. This book concentrates on trying to show what drove Sturt – his father being a British judge in India, his time as an officer in the army fighting in France, his arrival in Sydney with some soldiers in charge of a party of convicts, and his liking for Australia. It lacks the depth and objectivity of the first ranked book but is better at providing information for my focusing questions than the third ranked evidence.
3	*Great Explorers of Australia* edited by O. Sear. This is a collection of primary resources that includes diary entries, letters and extracts from journals. There is a large section on Sturt that contains interesting stories, such as a thermometer on the desert expedition measuring up to 53° C and then bursting. The information here is sketchier than that of the second ranked evidence but the stories are more colourful than that of the fourth ranked evidence and it relates better to my focusing questions. I will be able to use quotes from it to add colour and interest.

1 The following numbers were included in a student's ranking of 10 pieces of evidence. Beside each, put the number/s the student should mention in the reasons for ranking them that way.

a 3 ____________ b 4 ____________ c 7 ____________ d 10 ____________

2 a What are the two things you must mention when you make a ranking? ____________

b What is the relationship between ranking and focusing questions?

____

3 In the box, write or draw what *ranking historical information* means.

ISBN 9780170367141

UNIT 63
EVALUATING THE ENQUIRY

Historical investigation

After you have put your historical information, evidence and conclusions into the appropriate format and style, your last job is to evaluate it.

Some questions you can ask when you are evaluating your enquiry include:

> **evaluating** = looking at something carefully to work out its value and worth

What did I do that worked well?

What problems did I have?

Why were some things easier to do than others?

What did I like doing best?

What did I like doing least?

What was I most pleased about?

Did I find enough information to answer my focusing questions?

What, if anything, was I most disappointed about?

Was my information mostly useful, or mostly not useful?

What could I have done better?

What might I do differently next time?

What have I learnt about history skills?

What have I learnt about my skills?

What have I learnt about me?

1 Give a reason for each of the following.

a Evaluation is a useful skill to have.

____

____

b You need to be honest in your evaluation.

____

____

2 In each speech bubble, put a question that each student could ask during his or her evaluation. (five different questions)

3 In the box, write what *evaluation* means.

Answers

Unit 1

1 a Herodotus lived in Ancient Greece
  b Herodotus lived Before the Common Era (BCE)
  c Herodotus was an adult
  d He travelled around Greece and Persia to investigate the reasons for the war between the two countries

2 a Use a mobile phone b Use a GPS in the car
  c Complete homework on a computer
  d Watch DVDs or movies online

Unit 2

1 a Historical facts b Historical ideas

2 a (Example answer) When I was young, I watched the Beijing Olympics.
  b (Example answer) Earlier this year, I went to New Zealand.

3 (Example answer) Australia was a convict settlement; Demetre had Greek ancestors; Italy and Germany invaded Greece during the Second World War; Australian soldiers helped to defend Greece.

Unit 3

1 (Example answer) It is 2 p.m. on 23 April 2015 in Sydney, Australia. From that moment on (every second, minute and day) makes that time history because it is in the past.

2 2003 down to United States; 2011 down to Britain; 1804 down and across left to France; 1917 left to Russia; 1945 left to Japan; 2013 up and across left to Italy; 1770 up to Australia; 1959 up left to India; 1869 up left to Egypt; 1911 up to the South Pole; 2013 up right to South Africa; 2015 up and across to Australia; 1867 across right to United States.

Unit 4

1 Serbia and Bosnia-Herzegovina have disappeared from the 1925 map, as have the Ottoman Empire and the Austro-Hungarian Empire. New countries to appear are Finland, Estonia, Latvia, Lithuania, East Prussia, Poland, Czechoslovakia, Austria, Hungary, Yugoslavia, Turkey.

3 Russia and the Ukraine

Unit 5

1 a bodies b pottery c weapons

2 carbon dating and tree-ring dating (dendrochronology)

3 science and medicine

4 Archaeologists examine objects usually from societies that are pre-literate, that is, they have no written language. Historians examine written evidence.

Unit 6

1 (Example answer) My parents chose to become Australian citizens after they emigrated from South Africa.

2 WHY = swept away thousands of people; WHAT = tsunami; WHO = Meghna; WHEN = Boxing Day 2004; WHERE = island near Sumatra; HOW = clinging to a door

3 When, Where, Who

Unit 7

1 Examples could include: Taylor Swift; Cathy Freeman; Barak Obama; Tony Abbott; Ian Thorpe.

2 Types of people: childcare workers; engineers; hairdressers; interior decorators; nannies; optometrists; quality officers; real-estate agents; ushers; veterinary surgeons; waiters
Social history topics: kung-fu; ninjas; opera; quilts; units; vineyards; wine; x-ray machines; yachting; zoos

3 (Example answer) Rap music, surfing, Napoleon, Australian movies, the Wallabies, the Australian netball team, cars, Papua New Guinea, Aboriginal people, school uniforms

Unit 8

1 Events could include travel, holidays, an accident, an achievement, a sporting event

2 a Oral history makes older people feel valued
  b A personal account by someone who was there

3 a Parents, siblings, relatives, doctors and nurses
  b Anyone who watched it live on TV or was actually at the Olympics, or read about it in the newspaper

Unit 9

1 a Arriving late
  b Picking his nose, which is considered rude behaviour
  c Didn't ask permission to record before the interview
  d Not well prepared
  e Impolite, inconsiderate comment on the interviewee's age
  f Arguing with the interviewee
  g Has only asked Yes/No questions to which the interviewee cannot elaborate
  h Has not brought all necessary equipment

Unit 10

1 Essentially any other services besides those named on the drawing, e.g. babysitting, pest eradication, swimming lessons, tree pruning, car pooling.

2 (Example answer) My home is in a small community that has an hotel, a hall and a petrol station that also sells some frozen foods. Our nearest town, which has services like Ari's local community, is 25 km away.

3 a For example, a war memorial
  b It remembers and commemorates those who died in war in the service of their country.

Unit 11

1 A landline telephone; a TV; electric heaters; DVDs; keys

2 (Example answer) My toys are electronic and use batteries

3 a Present date minus 1880
  b For acts of bravery in war
  c To sell overseas and make money
  d It is to control Australia's national cultural heritage, to make sure it is preserved

Unit 12

1 a (Example answer) Eurovision Song Contest; World Cup Final; Olympic Games
  b Photographs; newspaper reports

2 From top: P, S, P, P, S, S, P, S, P, P

Unit 15

1 B 2 A

Unit 16

1 a 28 April 1994 b Elections and voting c Rugby Union
  d It is one of South Africa's major national sports; there were major apartheid protests at the 1971 Springbok rugby union tour of Australia
  e Black majority government

Unit 17

1 Kasi should have only given one piece of evidence; Jeni should have given an approximate distance; Von should have only referred to Source B; Adoni should have quoted the sentence, not rewritten it; Raz should have written an essay of 300–400 words; Jac should have written the essay using facts about why apartheid began; Sanjay should have focused on Australia's nuclear policy

Unit 18

1 Circle: treaty (Treaty), versailles (Versailles), WW1 (World War I or the First World War), p (annoyed, angered), Krauts (Germans), off (delete/slang), (should be full stop at end of sentence), this (This), Especially (especially), have (had), reps (representatives), which (that), president (President), wilson (Wilson), kind of (delete) league (League), nations (Nations), piece (peace), for ever, (forever.), they (They), responsibility (responsible), ww1 (WWI or the First World War), & (and), Gm (Germany) lotsa (a lot of, much) dough (money), Gm (Germany), it's (its), kolonys (colonies), was (were), countrys (countries), Forbid (Germany was forbidden), etc (and other weaponry)

Unit 19

1 a D b G c E d E
2 G = c; E = a; E = b

Unit 20

2 1 arrow to 'Veni, vidi, vici.'; 2 arrow to 'There is a homely adage which runs: …'; 3 arrow to full stop after 'vici'; 4 arrow to "Speak softly and carry a big stick: you will go far."'; 5 arrow to '… we shall fight'; 6 arrow to 'There is many a boy …'; 7 arrow to 'Veni, vidi, vici'; 8 arrow to [I came, I saw, I conquered.]

Unit 21

1 a They are books of fiction. b They are stories, not topics.
2 Following a set structure makes it easier to write, read and mark an essay.
4 Each sentence makes a point, so each sentence should have a tick. This gives the grade of A. The essay scores a 10 because it follows the rules of structure by having a clearly defined head (the first paragraph), a body (paragraphs 2, 3, 4, 5) and a tail (paragraph 6).

Unit 22

1 a place of publication b publisher
c place of publication
2 To indicate where the ideas, quotes and diagrams/photos came from; to acknowledge sources

Unit 23

1 a It is set out in alphabetical order
b Words and terms come first and are in bold
c Meanings alongside terms are as brief as possible
d There are no full stops because the sentences are incomplete sentences
2 The 'i' in indigenous is not capitalised; the definitions for the words peasant and polygamy have been mixed up; Urbanisation should be after Terrorism
3 'Balance of power' goes after Armistice; 'Minority' goes after Indigenous; 'Standard of living' goes after Reform (some students will later change their answer to 'after Revolution' and both are correct), 'Ethnic group' goes after Coup d'état, 'Revolution' goes after Reform, 'Fascism' goes after Exile
4 (Example answer for book about surfing) **Goofyfoot** rider who leads with right foot; **Lip** fringing crest of wave

Unit 24

1 a To create a feel-good coincidence
b Many people accepted the story and did not question it because they had no evidence to challenge it.
2 a Evie and Bella
b They could search the Internet for information or go to the library and read a book on the Second World War and the Holocaust.

Unit 25

1 (Example answer) In a discussion about climate change
2 Photographs, newspaper reports, official reports, government announcements, film clips, newsreels, personal accounts (oral history)

Unit 26

1 Discussion = 3, Report = 2, Review = 5, Speech = 1, Seminar = 6, Recorded conversation = 4
2 Debate, role play, multimedia presentation (e.g. PowerPoint) (these last two are also performance evidence)

Unit 27

1 a white b American Indians
c white d white people
2 Reports, newspapers, logbooks, diaries, websites
3 a A journal is a daily record of events and a logbook is a record of progress in achieving something.
b Oral evidence is spoken evidence, such as in a courtroom, whereas written evidence is information recorded on paper.

Unit 28

1 a Practical demonstration b sketch
c PowerPoint presentation d slide show
2 A dance production

Unit 29

2 France exploded four bombs in the Pacific as part of a test; the response to the French exploding bombs in the Pacific is a threat to test volcanoes in Paris.

Unit 30

1 a A cartoon b TransTasman Trade Tightrope
c Australian and New Zealand
d The two countries that are on the opposite sides of the Tasman Sea are New Zealand and Australia.
e The two figures are walking towards each other holding on to a tightrope that is not joined in the middle, but each man is holding an end.
f If the figure drops his rope, he will fall with it.
g The two countries do not always agree on issues/they are largely 'feeling their way' on issues
h One country is dominant/one country is trying to dominate

Unit 33

1 a right for the times b wrong for the times
c suitable for the event d formal
e classical f short

Unit 34

2 The last sentence in each is especially important

ISBN 9780170367141

Unit 35

1 **Beatles box:** people = fans and the Beatles, place = Darwin, period = 1964; **Captain Scott box:** people = Captain Scott and Captain Oates, place = South Pole, period = 1912; **Singapore box:** people = people in Singapore and people working for Wrigley, place = Singapore, period = 2004; **Europe box:** people = Japanese fighters, US bomber, the President, place = the USA and Japan, period = 1945

Unit 36

1 a All sentences in all caps should be underlined
 b All other boxes without all caps sentences
 c The First World War . . . = People had not seen what damage . . .; People used to believe . . . = They had no scientific instruments . . .; In 1955 . . . = A law banned black . . .; In the Middle Ages . . . = People were used to burning . . .; In 1918 . . . = The country was in . . .

Unit 37

2 a Mel has experienced the stress from war and she does not want the peace she enjoys in the park to be disturbed.
 b The uranium mine will bring new jobs and Stefano is looking for a job.
 c Parri is against uranium mining and fears that it will not be used for peaceful purposes but to make nuclear bombs. She also fears leaks into the environment, which may have an impact upon her future.

Unit 38

1 (Example answers) Sister, brother, friend, class captain, babysitter, stepson, cousin, etc.
2 (Example answer) Survivor = heartfelt, begging, emotional, desperate, insistent

Unit 39

1 Muslims working to get rights = Muslim League; Aboriginal and Torres Strait Islanders in Australia = Land Rights; Women = Suffrage; In America non-communists = McCarthyism; People who wanted the colonies = Federation; Protesters working to stop = Anti-war; German Nazis = Hitler Youth; Italians = Young Italy; People who did not believe = Anti-slavery; People who want = Peace; Groups working to get alcohol banned = Temperance; Settlers = Sons of Liberty; World-wide = Anti-apartheid; People against nuclear power = Anti-uranium; Indians = Satyagraha
2 Muslims, rights for Muslims; Aboriginal and Torres Strait Islanders, keep their land; Women and men, get women the right to vote; Non-communists, loyal to the United States; People who want colonies joined, federation and unity; Protesters against Vietnam war, to get Australia out of war; Nazis, young people to be loyal Nazis; Italians, joined together; People who did not believe in slavery, get rid of slavery; People who want world peace, get rid of weapons of mass destruction; Groups, get alcohol banned; Settlers, get rid of British; World-wide groups, get rid of separation of races; People against nuclear power, Australia not to mine its uranium resources; Indians, get rid of British rule

Unit 40

1 'in relation to'
2 a (Example answers) Went to one of the earliest screenings of *The Hobbit*
 b I bought my ticket well in advance
 c Because I wanted to be one of the first people on the planet to see the film by Peter Jackson
3 a to learn all I could about the *Aichi D3A2* (Val) aircraft, which did the dive bombing; I lost many mates from the sunken and destroyed ships and I wanted to know everything about the people who killed them.
 b to cut the story out of the newspaper; I wanted to add it to my file of great Australian cricketing moments and I was proud an Aussie had been given such an honour.

Unit 41

1 a communism b nationalism c industrialisation
 d democracy e religion f racism g multiculturalism
 h feminism i internationalism j fascism

Unit 42

1 a (Answers as of 2015) $4 b $3 c $10 d 20 cents
 e 5 cents f 30 cents
2 Your work is historically accurate if you use the conventions of the time.

Unit 43

1 First box = second sentence; second box = fourth sentence; third box = second sentence, fourth box = fourth sentence

Unit 44

1 Place a cross next to c and d
2 a Teachers b To report on my progress c Created as planned process d Written by my teachers who know me e Created to be private f Because they teach me, my teachers know how I behave and what achievement standards I have reached g The information is recorded in the teachers' student files during the term

Unit 45

1 a The driver glanced at Hitler and accidently headed over the bank.
 b In an effort to kill a bee, Ben Hur accidentally drove his chariot into a tree.
 c Friar Tuck had been travelling on horseback for three months. One day he fell asleep and crashed his horse.
 d After the President watched the chimp perform, the animal was taken to Queen Street and fed two buckets of bananas.
 e A lot of students were present when Sue Smith visited the school and lectured on 'Nasty Pests'.
 f The Governor-General smashed the champagne against the prow of the ship at the launching and the crowd cheered as the ship slid down the runway into the tide.
 g The protestors, who released the rats in Parliament, were arrested when they left.
 h There was a lot of violence at the Supreme Court.

Unit 46

1 Cross out 'should not have'
2 Opinions = He should have been made Sir Douglas before 1914; it is fitting that his face appears on the $100 note; all the others are facts

Unit 47

1 a atom bomb b boy with a cap c boy with a gun
 d camera

Unit 48

1 f, j, e, c, a, g, b, h, d, i

Unit 49

1 Quote something funny or wise box = arrow to 'I agree completely with my son . . .; Telling stories about the person box = arrow to 'It was reported he won $24 million playing blackjack . . .'; Write how people at the time box = arrow to 'media'; Use the measurements box = arrow to '1.90 m and 127 kg.'; Write the truth box = arrow to 'He also suffered from dyslexia'; Use formal language box = arrow to any sentence; Say where the person lived box = arrow to paragraph 2; Say if the person is survived by box = arrow to paragraph 1; Give date of death box = arrow to 26 December 2005; Give date of birth box = 17 December 1937; Say who box = arrow to first sentence

Unit 50

1 a BCE, CE
 b pre-history, ancient history, the Dark Ages, the Middle Ages, Renaissance, modern history
 c decade, score, century
 d biennial, octennial, decennial, sesquicentennial, millennial
2 a 200th b 17th c 700th d 15 000th

Unit 51

2 1900, 1904, 1908, 1912, 1920, 1924, 1928, 1932, 1952, 1956, 1960, 1968, 1976, 1980, 1984, 1992, 1996, 2012, 2016 (1916 cancelled due to the First World War, 1940 and 1944 cancelled due to the Second World War)

Unit 52

1 Tourists caught in the disaster; donating money; sending experts, including medical staff to help with the injured
2 The first sentence

Unit 54

1 Top left to right = 3, 7, 4, 2; bottom left to right = 1, 6, 5, 8

Unit 55

1 Defining, making up questions, planning, gathering, selecting, keeping a log, organising, ranking, using appropriate format and style, evaluating
2 *History Skills* has bite-sized units on important history skills so it answers all my five focusing questions. I will use it as the basis of my investigation and find examples from my chosen specialist topic (Australian exploration) to go with each skill.

Unit 56

1 Underline = 1948 communists; Malaya tried to take over; Britain ruled Malaya; communists camps jungle; ambushed traffic; derailed trains; hit-and-run raids; killed owners of rubber plantations; burned factories; cut rubber trees; British platoons fought communists; used cunning; example can of food punctured

 Notes = 1948 communists Malaya rebelled ag Brit rulers. Coms had jungle camps. Ambushed, derailed, raided, killed, burned, cut trees. Brit plats fought & used cunning e.g. canned fd punctured.
2 a British b for example c communists
3 In 1948, Malayan communists rebelled.

Unit 57

1 a, b, e, g

Unit 58

1 a focus b focusing
2 Cross out b

Unit 59

1 a to look ahead b suited to the individual student

Unit 60

1 Collected, chose, numbered, made note in log

Unit 61

1 a Alphabetical order of titles for information, shortest pieces of information to longest pieces of information
 b (Example answer) I would choose the option that Zac used because it seems the most logical and if I label everything carefully, this option would still let me be totally organised.
2 a Dai had decided right at the beginning on a system of organising his information and stuck to it
 b Dai will know how to organise things so that the job runs smoothly.

Unit 62

1 a 2 and 4 b 3 and 5 c 6 and 8 d 9 and 11
2 a You must give the reason why you ranked one piece of evidence above another piece of evidence and why you ranked it below another piece of evidence.
 b The ranking of evidence should reflect how closely they answer the focusing questions.

Unit 63

1 a Being able to critically analyse will help in all aspects of life
 b Pretending that something is fine when it is not means you never improve
2 (Example answers) What did I most like doing? What could I have done better? Why did I not get my work finished on time? Why did I end up with so much irrelevant information? Why did I find this work so easy to organise?

ISBN 9780170367141